EDUCA

Concise, engaging and accessible, *Education Research: The Basics* discusses key ideas about the nature and purpose of education research: what it can and cannot achieve, how it has been used in the past and where and how it has an impact.

Providing crucial insight into the work of education researchers, this book:

- Offers seven chapters, each representing a way of understanding the goals and methods of research conducted in the field
- Considers key thinkers in the field, such as Plato, Hirsch, Dewey, Montessori and Freire
- Explores case studies from a range of perspectives
- Provides key terms and further reading throughout

The perfect pocket resource to dip into, *Education Research: The Basics* provides accessible support for those studying education as a subject, for practitioners concerned with developing their practice and for anyone who wants to know more about education and how it is researched.

Michael Hammond leads an MA in social science research and is Reader in Education at the University of Warwick, UK.

Jerry Wellington was a Professor and Head of Research Degrees in the School of Education at the University of Sheffield, UK, and is now an educational consultant.

THE BASICS SERIES

The Basics is a highly successful series of accessible guidebooks which provide an overview of the fundamental principles of a subject area in a jargon-free and undaunting format.

Intended for students approaching a subject for the first time, the books both introduce the essentials of a subject and provide an ideal springboard for further study. With over 50 titles spanning subjects from artificial intelligence (AI) to women's studies, *The Basics* are an ideal starting point for students seeking to understand a subject area.

Each text comes with recommendations for further study and gradually introduces the complexities and nuances within a subject.

For a full list of titles in this series, please visit www.routledge.com/The-Basics/book-series/B

EDUCATION RESEARCH

THE BASICS

**MICHAEL HAMMOND WITH
JERRY WELLINGTON**

Routledge
Taylor & Francis Group

LONDON AND NEW YORK

First published 2020
by Routledge
2 Park Square, Milton Park, Abingdon, Oxon, OX14 4RN

and by Routledge
52 Vanderbilt Avenue, New York, NY 10017

Routledge is an imprint of the Taylor & Francis Group, an informa business

British Library Cataloguing-in-Publication Data
A catalogue record for this book is available from the British Library

Library of Congress Cataloging-in-Publication Data
Names: Hammond, Mike, author. | Wellington, J. J. (Jerry J.) author.
Title: Education research : the basics / Mike Hammond with Jerry Wellington.
Description: Abingdon, Oxon ; New York, NY : Routledge, 2020. | Includes bibliographical references.
Identifiers: LCCN 2019008740| ISBN 9781138386761 (hardback) | ISBN 9781138386792 (pbk.) | ISBN 9780429426629 (ebooks)
Subjects: LCSH: Education–Research. | Education–Philosophy.
Classification: LCC LB1028 .H31145 2020 | DDC 370.72–dc23
LC record available at https://lccn.loc.gov/2019008740

ISBN: 978-1-138-38676-1 (hbk)
ISBN: 978-1-138-38679-2 (pbk)
ISBN: 978-0-429-42662-9 (ebk)

Typeset in Bembo and Bliss
by Wearset Ltd, Boldon, Tyne and Wear

CONTENTS

TABLES

ACRONYMS AND INITIALISMS

AfL	Assessment for learning
CoP	Community of practice
ER	Educational research
ICT	Information and communication technology
IRF/E	Initiation, response, feedback, evaluation
IWB	Interactive whiteboard
MBA	Master of Business Administration
MOOC	Massive Online Open Courses
NGO	Non-governmental organisation
NPD	National Pupil Database
OECD	Organisation for Economic Co-operation and Development
PISA	The Programme for International Student Assessment
RCT	randomised control trial
SES	Socioeconomic status
VLE	virtual learning environment

INTRODUCTION

The aim of this book is to give the reader insight into the work of education researchers. It looks at how education research is carried out; the purposes it serves; how the research literature can be read; and what kind of themes researchers cover. It is suitable for anyone studying education as a subject, for practitioners concerned with developing their practice and for the general reader who simply wants to know more about education and how it is researched.

The book is organised around a series of chapters that cover: *addressing* problems of practice; *generalising* about education; *describing and categorising* actions and strategies; *explaining and theorising* in education; *advocating* educational change. A seventh chapter looks at the contribution of education research and sets out some present day challenges. The book reads best in sequence with the final chapter providing a reflection on what has gone on before.

We now describe each chapter in more detail. This introduction gives an overview of the book. The book proper begins with Chapter 2 in which we look at research carried out by practitioners in order to address practical problems of teaching and learning. This research often falls under the banner of action research and we look at the strengths and limitations of action research as well as other approaches such as classroom study and reflective practice.

We introduce three case studies to illustrate the action research tradition and look at other approaches to practice research including lesson study and action learning. In this chapter we look too at research methods including observation, interviewing and focus groups.

In Chapter 3 we move to a very different research tradition, one offering generalisations about education very often based on the precise measurement of learning outcomes. We begin by looking at randomised control trials (RCTs), which show differences between groups who have access to an intervention and those that do not. We introduce further research methods including meta-analyses and systematic reviews, we outline how comparisons are made by measuring strength of correlation and effect sizes. We take in international comparisons in student outcomes in the work carried out by The Programme for International Student Assessment (PISA). Finally, we look at recent developments in Big Data research. Attempts to generalise about education give us a big picture but a limitation is that we can lose sight of the detail of classroom life.

In Chapter 4 we look at smaller scale studies that aim to provide this detail. We illustrate the importance of categorising what we see (e.g. observations), what we hear (e.g. classroom talk) and what we are told (e.g. interviews). Through categorising it is possible to compare and contrast different classrooms and to see the consequences of actions for teachers and students. We introduce studies on teacher questioning, classroom talk and school leadership and conclude with a note on the varied nature of teacher knowledge.

In Chapter 5 we look back at the previous chapters by discussing the different kinds of explanations put forward in education research. We recognise the contributions from different types of research tradition including: small-scale case study; practice research; large-scale meta-analysis and systematic review. Each approach comes with distinctive strengths and limitations and we argue that using a variety of approaches will give us a fuller picture. We also introduce the idea of theorising about education as a way of organising ideas around more abstract concepts. Here we discuss the different meanings given to theory and we see the benefit of theorising as offering greater transferability. Finally, we look at interdisciplinary research. We conclude that while researchers can learn from other disciplines, education research has a distinctive concern for addressing practical problems.

In Chapter 6 we move on to look at those advocating change in how education is organised and how teachers do their work. We look at six kinds of advocacy: neoliberal; conservative; liberal; reformist, progressive and radical. The first two of these are often seen as politically conservative, sceptical of the role of the state in education and in favour of a more directed, deductive form of teaching. However, there are important differences. Neoliberals focus more on the organisation of systems and the importance of free markets, while conservatives are more interested in cultural aspects of education, in particular the protecting of a common culture that can be handed down across generations. Liberal educationalists, meanwhile, see the wider goal of education as a preparation for living a good life while reformers concentrate their arguments on developing a more appropriate curriculum, one that carries greater creativity and relevance. Progressives are concerned to recognise the rights of the child and see education as a natural unfolding while radicals draw attention to inequality in society and want education to play a role in addressing this.

Chapter 7 looks back at the book at a whole. We recognise the varied nature of education research both in terms of what is studied and the methods used to study it, but argue that education researchers have a distinctive interest in how we can help learners to go from one way of understanding culture, society or the physical world to one that is better. We reaffirm the importance of education and the value of education and set out some of the things that education research tells us. Finally, we raise six challenges for those conducting education research today.

Each chapter is organised into sections. We begin with a general introduction and a signpost to what follows. We then include sections on the key themes and add a brief summary. Within each chapter, we cite sources that will help those wanting to go deeper into particular issues but we have avoided over-referencing in order not to disrupt the text. We offer, too, a guide to further reading at the end of the chapter and here we have tried to select one or two of the more accessible texts, often ones that are freely available online. In each chapter, including in this introduction, there are key words that are listed in an extensive glossary at the back of the book.

We have written this book as we believe education matters. Education provides opportunities for better economic prospects and allows us as individuals to make more informed decisions as to how we want to lead our lives. We hope that by reading this book you will get a better idea about education research, how to read it critically, how to conduct it intelligently and how to contribute to wider discourse. We ask questions as to the nature of educational research, what it can and cannot achieve, how it has been carried out over the years, where and why it has had an impact. We discuss some of the questions that have pre-occupied education researchers for many years such as: *What does good or effective teaching and learning look like? Why do some students achieve higher learning outcomes than others? What is special about educational research? How and why should students be assessed? What is the difference between informal and formal learning and which is more effective? Can practitioners carry out their own research? What relationship should teachers have with literature? Is there any such thing as a learning style? What does successful group work look like? Does progressive education represent a better or worse alternative to what many experience in school?* However, we are exemplifying these debates, we are not offering a comprehensive guide to each and every issue. In similar vein we cannot in a short book like this cover every context in which education takes place. We do present as wide a variety of contexts as we can, for example leadership in schools in Vietnam; classroom talk in England; early years education in Italy; the apprenticeship of tailors in Liberia; future studies in higher education in Germany. And, as far as it is natural to do so, we talk about the work of *practitioners* as well as teachers to indicate that we are interested in many different roles in education – lecturer, instructor, teaching assistant, administrator, mentor, trainer and so on – and we refer to *students* to cover early years and school aged children as well as learners in post-compulsory settings. When we refer to classrooms, these could be teaching spaces in school, seminar rooms in university or nursery settings. But we cannot cover everything. For example, we do not deal with the teaching of particular subjects; we mention, but do not say enough about students with special needs; there is a lot more we could have said about arts education; and we have not discussed in detail the growing role of home education. We have consciously sought to include references and examples from different countries and raise the concept of decolonising education, but our references are skewed towards the literature and contexts we know best. Finally, the book describes many of the research methods that education researchers use including interviews, observation, surveys and various forms of data analysis including coding and descriptive and inferential statistics. However, it is not a comprehensive 'Research Methods' book – there are many books that offer this and some we cite in our further reading sections. We want to give you the wider picture.

Most people, certainly policy makers, have something to say about education as they have endured, or even enjoyed, considerable exposure to schooling and post-school study. By introducing some of the key debates about education and giving you insight into the tools of the education researcher, we hope this book helps you see your educational experiences, and perhaps engage in your own research project, from a wider perspective.

We would like to thank students and colleagues for their suggestions about this book and Penny Nunn for reading each chapter closely. All mistakes, and errors of omission, are, of course, our own.

2

PRACTITIONERS ADDRESSING PROBLEMS OF PRACTICE

INTRODUCTION

We start with the practitioners, the teachers, lecturers, instructors, assistants, mentors and so on who make education work. Where do they fit into the field of education research? One answer is that they can be the instruments of research themselves, they can become the people who carry out research and they can use their research to assist them in their work. Such research carried out by practitioners often falls under the umbrella term of action research and in this chapter we describe action research, we discuss its strengths and the tensions that come with it and raise some of the criticisms made of it. We go on to introduce other approaches to practitioner led research and introduce some well used tools for education research and draw out some talking points along the way.

ACTION RESEARCH

When practitioners carry out their own research this is often described as action research. The term action research is thought to have been first used by Kurt Lewin in his work on improving understanding of minority groups in USA during the second world war (1939–45). Lewin, (1997 [1951]) himself did not work with teachers or schools but his ideas were taken up in education. Over the intervening years action research has gone in and out of popularity.

Educational action research has been defined in different ways and there are different models for carrying it out – for example, McNiff (2016); Stringer, McFadyen and Baldwin (2010); Winter (1989). However, a recurring idea is that it describes a systematic attempt by practitioners to address a practical problem through cycles of planning, implementing and reflecting. To go into this more deeply, practitioners could include teachers, lecturers, teaching assistants but they could also be school leaders, university administrators, health workers, community workers, advisors and in fact anyone whose work involves education in the broad sense of the word. The problems action researchers face are varied as they are identified by the practitioners themselves; this is bottom up research *by* practitioners for improving practice, not top down research carried out *on* practitioners. As such, action research usually begins with asking 'How can I do this better?' type questions. For example:

- How can I best support new arrivals in my class?
- How can I help my staff to be more collegiate?
- How can I work with young offenders to get them back into work?
- How can I best use Interactive Whiteboards (IWBs) in my classroom?

These types of question signal a concern for addressing practical problems and a belief that there is something that can be done about these problems even if the scope for change is limited and interventions always come with unexpected consequences. Once having framed a question to address a problem, action researchers might follow cycles of action and reflection, which we describe here under the headings of **reconnaissance**, **design, implementation** and **evaluation**. We look at these stages of a project in more detail.

RECONNAISSANCE

Most projects begin with an attempt to investigate a problem more deeply. This is sometimes reported as a reconnaissance phase. For example, a teacher, let us call her teacher X, might ask herself 'why are some of my pupils disengaged in class?'. X may then set about trying to get a better perspective on the problem, for example by finding out how colleagues have addressed disengagement in their lessons and asking if they have any ideas for what might work in her class. X may find out, say, how other teachers worked at giving clearer directions to their students when setting up small group activities or how they have provided 'just in time' feedback (i.e. feedback at the point at which it is needed) so that students are not left to flounder. Other teachers might have ideas about the use of support materials to make abstract ideas more accessible, for example the use of base 10 cubes (these are generally wooden or plastic bricks in sizes of single cubes; blocks of 10; blocks of 100) to physically represent place value in mathematics or virtual reality representations (for example recreations of prehistoric worlds) to stimulate discussion of natural selection in science. At this stage X might not only talk to other teachers but observe lessons or parts of lessons as well as visit other schools.

In carrying out this reconnaissance most practitioners put a higher value on ideas that they can see used in a local context; they want to know that an intervention will work with their students in their school (or other educational institution) and are often sceptical as to whether what works elsewhere is transferable to their classroom. However, they can expand their knowledge of available interventions through teacher discussion forums, subject association conferences and practice literature. Academic literature should be influential too but it is frequently found inaccessible to practitioners and indeed a recurring frustration, which we return to later, is that many practitioners find such literature remote from their concerns both in style and content. In contrast, academics, themselves, often feel frustrated when the insights they offer are ignored not just by policy makers but practitioners. All is not lost. Academic literature does tend to inform action research when the practitioner researcher is undertaking some kind of accredited programme such as a masters degree or working in partnership with outside agencies. Academic findings are often shared in school if there are other colleagues undertaking post-degree learning of their own.

DESIGN

Once the action researcher has identified possible interventions to address their problem, they will weigh up the predicted opportunities and constraints within each and then design an intervention. This design will usually cover a timetable for the intervention, the nature of the intervention and the way the intervention is to be evaluated. Sometimes this will include a SWOT analysis. A SWOT analysis is a matrix used to help a person or organisation identify the Strengths, Weaknesses, Opportunities and Threats related, in this case, to an intervention. Its roots are in business planning but it can be used as a more general planning tool. For example, in the case of a using a new idea in teaching, say the use of group work, a teacher might identify:

Strengths: my recent and relevant teacher training; my interest in more cooperative approaches; the promotion of group work in my department.

Opportunities: to use group work to make my classes more interesting for students; to allow students to discuss their ideas and learn from others.

Weaknesses: my lack of experience in using group work for teaching purposes; students seeing group work as an opportunity to go off-task rather than engage in learning; uncertainty about support in my school as a whole.

Threats: not enough time to plan this properly; negative feedback from school leadership

In this reconnaissance phase it would be surprising if the teacher did not try to 'test the water'. For example, X, who was looking to engage pupils in her lessons, may decide that there were some innovative ideas in group work, for example so-called jigsaw groupings, in which students are put into initial groups but then later report back to their peers within new groups, which might be worth trying out in advance of a full blown intervention. She would then learn not only more about whether the planned intervention would be well received but also if she felt comfortable about teaching in this way.

In the design phase action researchers plan for both implementation and evaluation. It is the focus on evaluation that makes action research more systematic than everyday professional learning. Indeed, many practitioners spend a great deal of time and energy thinking about how to do their work better, and go on to try out new ideas and reflect on how they got on. However, they rarely do this as systematically as in an action research project. In the design phase the practitioner will think about the aims of his or her project and how to access data to assess how far these aims were met. This might involve covering the ABC of evaluation: Attitudes (or affective) responses; Behavioural changes; and Cognitive gains (i.e. what students learnt) springing from the intervention. A key challenge in carrying out evaluation is that action researchers are participant observers, that is they are taking part in the everyday life of the institution while trying to record what is happening. This has the considerable advantage of giving the researcher the 'whole picture' of the context they are researching and it also gives opportunity for informal interaction or 'ethnographic conversations' with students. However, participant observation is taxing and it can muddy expectations of roles in an organisation.

IMPLEMENTATION

The next phase of an action research project is that of implementation. The implementation phase is often briefly described in an action research project and might consist of a time line with key events mapped out with notes of any changes of approach as the project got underway. For example, our teacher X may list a series of attempts to use formative assessment during her lesson and report on what happened on each occasion. Things become more complicated if the teacher undergoes a change of direction during the action research. This is quite possible if she can see the intervention is not working or that there is a better alternative. In this case the action researcher should chart when and why this change came about and provide the evidence on which the decision to change was based. The description of the implementation should also include the methods used and a diary of key events.

EVALUATION

The systematic evaluation of a project is complicated and the evaluation phase can be challenging. Self-evaluation is very important. For example, many action research projects involve attempts to improve a teacher's knowledge, confidence and sense of efficacy and it would be essential for the action researcher to ask him or herself, 'How did I feel using these ideas in practice?'. Subjective responses can be quickly recorded in a research diary during or after a lesson, though the longer this is left the more difficult it is to recall what you were feeling at the time. However, when it comes to student responses the teacher cannot rely only on intuition and feeling, more objective approaches are needed. For example, in order to access student attitudes, the teacher may want to carry out quick pre- and post-intervention survey or conduct interviews, more often focus groups, with their students. They might broaden the evaluation by inviting teacher colleagues into their classroom and asking for their comments on how the intervention is being received by the students.

EVALUATION TOOLS

It is worth saying more about surveys, interviews and observation at this point, for not only are they widely used in action research but they are also standard research tools in many other approaches to education research.

The point of a survey is to find out how many feel, think or behave in a particular way and surveys provide the general picture relatively quickly and easily. A great deal has been written on the design of questionnaires. Designers need a clear awareness of the concepts they are researching and the kinds of questions that will provide a suitable means of measurement. For example, surveys often start with straightforward, closed questions, leaving the open-ended, and 'matter of opinion' questions to the end. Several types of scale can be used, including binary options (yes/no) but also Likert scales for agreement (for example do you strongly agree/agree/disagree/strongly disagree that sport should be compulsory in this school?) and frequency (do you/always/sometimes/often/seldom/never take part in organised sport at the weekend).

Most textbooks on research methods (for example Cohen, et al., 2011; Hammond and Wellington, 2013; Punch & Oancea, 2014; Wellington, 2015) stress the importance of asking unambiguous 'value free' questions; appreciating that people will not invest much time in completing surveys; and presenting a survey as attractively as possible. Unlike the interview, the survey is fixed and a great deal of time needs to be invested in clarifying exactly what the researcher wants to find out and how to measure it. Again, the small-scale action researcher has an advantage here as they can often be present during the completion of the survey and can clarify anything that is not understood.

One of the key issues in using a survey involves sampling – though this may be much less of an issue for action researchers if they are trying to get feedback from everyone in a class. Sampling might be random, for example every fifth person on a randomly organised list of students, or a definite decision might be made to 'stratify' the sample according to certain criteria, e.g. gender, age, ethnicity. If a sample is used the researcher should be able to say how and why it is representative. Response rates are another challenge though again in a small-scale action research project surveys can often be given out to a 'captive population'. However ethical issues will arise and students should not be expected to take part if they have not given permission (or in the case of younger students parental permission has not been given). Needless to say, having some students not taking part can skew the data.

In good survey research, researchers have a close relationship to the data. They understand how the questions were generated, they have addressed the problems exposed in piloting, and they are aware of the likely spread of responses, which provides a credibility check on the plethora of descriptive and inferential statistics that can be automatically generated using software packages.

The survey typically 'goes wide' and to go deeper into student responses the researcher might carry out interviews with a sample of students and focus group discussions. Here data can be very time consuming to collect and analyse and it is easy to see how the size and sophistication of data collection makes the evaluation of an action research more systematic and detailed than interventions carried in the normal course of teaching.

The value of the interview is that it allows you to probe a student's account of an event as well as their thoughts, values, feelings and perspectives more generally. Interviews 'go deep' allowing the researcher to see an event or context from the point of view of the people he or she is researching; interviews are interactive in ways in which questionnaires are not; the researcher can provide clarification of questions and follow unexpected responses. Creating an interview schedule involves turning an area of inquiry into a set of questions that are easy for the student, or other interviewee, to follow. Interviews involve careful use of language e.g. avoidance of jargon, and clarity in phrasing. Interviews are often broken down by type. The structured interview may be little more than a 'face-to-face questionnaire' and can be of value when more than one teacher is working on the same project. At the opposite end of the spectrum, an 'unstructured' interview will be far less predictable, what is covered will vary from one interview to the next. In some cases, it may be possible to start with one single, key question to act as a trigger. Semi-structured interviews may be more manageable than unstructured ones while avoiding the inflexibility of the fully structured approach. Group interviews or focus groups in which a researcher talks with (say) three, four or more students together can often have advantages. The students, or other interviewees, may feel more secure and at ease if they are with their peers. This may be an important consideration for practitioner researchers as a sole student may feel overwhelmed by the status of the practitioner as a figure of authority in the school or other institution. The disadvantages are also clear: groups can be swayed by more dominant members and it can be difficult to deduce the degree of agreement in the group as much is expressed implicitly. Action researchers wanting to use interviews or focus groups have the advantage of easy access to their students and the opportunity for informal conversations during the normal course of teaching. Some may find it challenging to step out of teacher role into a listener role and all should factor in that one way or another their presence may skew the conversation in particular ways. Here it is important to follow ethical guidelines.

Finally, observation, for example observation of lessons, can be taxing for experienced as well as novice researchers, even more so in practitioner research where you might have to teach a lesson and collect feedback at the same time. Here a critical friend is useful as they might record their observations using a schedule discussed in advance. Researchers in larger scale projects often record the lesson (after due ethical procedures have been agreed) and then play back the events and make observation notes. The key value of observation is that it deals with behaviour rather than reported behaviour. This is important as there may be a considerable mismatch between what we think happened, or what we thought we saw happening, and what really happened. As with interviews, observation can be structured or unstructured and often a mix of both, for example observers may use time lines to provide a structure with key events noted. Unstructured observation can be difficult to organise while overly structured observation may end up missing the important in favour of what is more easily recordable. Where possible, observation can be improved with peer feedback. Some researchers use a stimulated recall approach in order to discuss what they have seen with those they have observed.

There will be other forms of data, which can be examined after an intervention. For example, students may be asked in the natural course of the lesson to undertake tasks and tests and these can be compared pre- and post-intervention. In some contexts, it is quite common to ask students to carry out online activity such as participation in forums. These can be examined for the number and type of comments made by students including logs of who has accessed what, when and for what purpose. Teachers are increasingly using polling software inside classrooms and lecture halls, too. They can set up and display pages with multiple-choice options and students can select their response via a mobile phone, tablet or desk top computer. These short surveys can provide a check for understanding or feedback on specific issues. Responses are aggregated, using automatically generated charts, and displayed openly. However individual responses are anonymised allowing students to show gaps in their understanding without drawing attention to themselves. Of course, a less formal way of surveying opinion is to ask for a show of hands.

TENSIONS WITHIN ACTION RESEARCH

In principle it is difficult to be against action research as there is ample evidence that it can lead to increased confidence and a sense of efficacy among teachers, new experiences for learners and an impact on solving practical problems in the classroom. At a whole school level it can lead to a flowering of creativity and enterprise and a potential re-engaging of the work force and a culture of innovation and peer support. Yet there are some important tensions in the way we think about action research and some outright criticisms.

A first tension involves the modelling of action research. We have given one version (earlier) organised around a learning cycle involving identification of a problem, reconnaissance, implementation and evaluation. There are many variations offered in the literature on how to describe action research within these broad parameters. For example, Whitehead (1989), Elliot (1991) and McNiff (2016) have offered more iterative approaches conceiving of inquiry as a series of cycles within cycles. This has the advantage of reminding the researcher to be flexible and adaptive and addresses the danger in more linear approaches that the researcher becomes wedded to one version of action and follows it through no matter what. In contrast some action researchers want to get away from models altogether and ask the practitioner researcher simply to remember that they are trying to improve their work through putting ideas into practice in order to make their teaching, or other teaching related work, better.

A second tension in action research is whether the focus should be on problem or opportunity. Of course, you can do both, but there is a danger of seeing action research as reactive or remedial as if it was always about addressing problems. For example, working on opportunities may be particularly important for projects that involve new technology as ICT is often introduced into education without a specific purpose in mind – it offers a solution to an unasked question. Perhaps these opportunities are best explored in a class in which the practitioner feels comfortable rather than as with teacher X, in one that was causing her discomfort.

Third, there are models of action research that offer a more critical view of educational systems as against those that seek pragmatic change in teaching and learning as in the example of teacher X. These approaches often fall under the banner of critical action research (Carr & Kemmis, 1986) as they are aimed as much at understanding what is oppressive in teaching and learning as they are at ameliorating conditions – something we look at more closely in discussing radical perspectives on education in Chapter 6. However, even if their goal is pragmatic change, all action researchers need to have a realistic view of what difference they can make without the involvement of others and without changes in society. For example, there is growing evidence on the importance of educating girls in developing societies, both as a goal in its own right and also for the key role that girls play in family life and in economic development more generally (e.g. Karoui & Feki, 2018). However, it is not expected that girls attend school in some countries and in many countries parents may withdraw children as they have not the money to pay for travel or learning resources or more simply, they need their children to work. Action research can help address this, especially if carried out with the help of NGOs and appropriate government agencies, but clearly an individual teacher or indeed group of teachers can only do so much. A lot of discussion on the limits of action research coalesces around the question of what it means for action research to 'work'. All action research offers a step towards addressing problems but in some approaches the focus might be on understanding the limits of change or on the professional learning taking place, irrespective of the impact of the project. Good action research can open up understanding of institutions and society.

Fourth, with the third point in mind, there are models of action research that insist on a collaborative element, often involving practitioners at the same school and/or the involvement of project facilitators often from nearby higher education institutions. This becomes important when supporting teachers not only through the different phases of a project but also to address institutional wide consequences of their project. In fact, many institutional leaders are happy to support action research but they often seek to control the parameters of projects in ways in which they are more comfortable. Others can go along with change but lack the commitment to follow it through. Here we recall one action research project in which a teacher wanted to better address the support given to new arrivals in her tutor group (the tutor group was the class that she registered in the morning and offered pastoral and other support to), particularly those in families seeking asylum. She was aware these new arrivals might feel lost and even intimidated as they moved into a class in which relationships had already been formed and in addition they might carry memories of traumatic events as well as weak target language skills. She carefully looked at the literature on good practice, investigated policies in her school and others, she noted the importance of good communication between teachers, as well as between teachers and parents, and the need to be proactive in putting peer support in place. She also found it important to help many new arrivals access language support. Her intervention covered things she could do better with her own tutor group but she also set out well-argued recommendations for a whole school approach to new arrivals. In this case the school leaders were happy to accept these recommendations but inertia set in and nothing happened. This kind of experience is of course dispiriting for action researchers but not uncommon.

Fifth, some action researchers are keen to apply the principles of action learning that they found useful in their own professional learning in their teaching. This often falls under the banner of participatory action research – which at a minimum requires students to address their own problems and develop their own means of evaluation. Such participatory research often has an explicit ethical commitment to equity and learner 'empowerment'.

Finally, there are ethical dimensions to all action research projects. Ethical question not only cover relationships with students and with colleagues but what kinds of innovations are in the spirit of the action research tradition. Here we, the authors, can recall another project. This took place at a time when there was considerable focus on the percentage of passes a year group in a certain school was expected to achieved in national examinations. We discussed several action research projects to address exam performance and some of the teacher interventions focused on special help for 'borderline' students (those who could with intervention reach the required grade). This meant side-lining intervention work for 'weak students', who were seen as incapable of reaching a pass grade no matter what support was offered, or 'very good students', whose success was assured. It is not difficult to sympathise with teachers in constructing their response. However, it did seem to us, that with time and resources limited, that the support offered for some was at the expense of others and this was not really in the spirit of action research.

CRITICISMS OF ACTION RESEARCH

Outright criticism of action research generally focuses on the excessive demands being made on practitioners particularly in tackling areas such as educational evaluation in which they may have little past experience to draw upon. Reflection on learning may be second nature to most practitioners but full-blown action research is not a natural activity to undertake. Many will feel they have not the time or energy to commit themselves to undertaking their own research and indeed a lot of practitioners may not want to. They may feel happier in following top down direction from school leaders as long as such direction is based on firm evidence – though what is firm evidence? – or following what seems intuitively sensible. Perhaps the point here is that practitioners cannot be in a continual state of action research; its value is to develop a way of thinking about change and a sense of self-efficacy rather than formalised procedures to continuously follow.

Second, there are complaints by professional researchers that action research projects are often poorly described and difficult to generalise from. In one sense this is true as action researchers may feel under little pressure to generalise and, as a point of principle, may believe that, as all solutions are local, what works in their class might not work in the class next door. However, it is disappointing that there are not more attempts to bring out what has been learnt through action research as there is a wisdom of practice within so many projects that lies untapped.

REFLECTIVE PRACTICE AND OTHER PRACTICE LED APPROACHES

So far, we have written about action research in particular but other approaches to practitioner research have been put forward. For example, it is fashionable to write about teaching as a reflective practice and to see action research as a particularly systematic form of reflective practice. Like action research, reflective practice does not have a single meaning but its main idea is that to learn professionally you need to pay close attention to your day-to-day experiences and consider how to change things for the better. Again, it is based on a continuous cycle of experience, observation and reflection in which new ideas are tested and evaluated. Kolb (1984) has, for example, been influential in the fields of adult learning and adult professional development (see McGregor & Cartwright, 2011) and his model set around a cycle of 'concrete learning, reflective observation, abstract conceptualisation and active experimentation' has been often used. The key idea in reflective learning is that as a learner you move from experiencing an environment towards being an active agent in that environment; the learning cycle takes you from observer to doer. Gibbs (1988), again in the context of adult learning, put forward something similar, but put a greater emphasis on the feelings one might have about an event and how these feelings will lead you to reflect on events in particular ways. In all models of reflective practice reflection is a key term and is often used in conjunction with the idea of reflexivity. Reflection we are familiar with, it is thinking about events and making sense of them – though, to complicate things, reflective practitioners often distinguish between *reflection in action* and *reflection on action* drawing on ideas originally offered by Schön (1983). Reflection-in-action refers to 'thinking on your feet' and the way you can pick up in an everyday situation what might be going wrong and what you can do to correct it. For example, those who are very good at sport have mastery of a core set of skills but they also know how to change or adjust their game based on what their opponent is doing or the particular circumstances of that moment – they are very good at reflecting in action. Reflection-on-action is what happens afterwards – to pursue the sports analogy – understanding what led up to you winning or losing the game. In contrast, reflexivity takes place at a more abstract or what is often described as a meta-level. It refers not so much as to the judgements we make about our performance but what led us to think about problems in a certain way. A reflexive approach will involve exploring the influence of our past assumptions, the position we hold in an organisation and the influence of others on our thinking. In summary, reflective practice celebrates not only the professional knowledge that practitioners have gained through study and exposure to literature but the 'know how' they have developed in practice.

Much of what has been said earlier about action research in terms of strengths and criticisms also apply to reflective practice. However, some versions of reflective practice are more flexible and more accessible than action research and can be better embedded in everyday practice. On the other hand, some versions of reflective practice are so focused on the practitioner's learning that they can neglect the search for more objective evidence of impact.

LESSON STUDY

Another kind of reflective practice is the idea of lesson study. This is often seen as originating in Japan (see Yoshida, 1999) and popularised particularly in the USA through Stigler and Hiebert (1999) and others. As with action research, this is concerned with cycles of improvement in teaching and learning in which teachers work together to address problems, plan, implement and evaluate change. While action research can take many forms, and can be carried out by anyone with a professional interest in education in its broadest sense, lesson study, as the name suggests, is focused on classroom teaching and learning. It is framed as a collaborative approach. Teachers get together to plan a research lesson and with one team member teaching and others gathering evidence on student learning and development. The team meets afterwards to reflect on the lesson, seek improvements in the design of the lesson and perhaps follow a new cycle of implementation and shared evaluation. It is, like reflective practice, more focused on teacher development than conventional problem solving action research. Its collaborative nature introduces a rigour to evaluation but the evaluation process can be less formal than full scale action research.

ACTION LEARNING

Action learning is more usually seen as an approach to organisational learning than to teaching in particular. The concept is often credited to original work by Revans (1982). The idea is, again as in action research, to solve real life problems by taking action and reflecting upon the results. As with lesson study it often calls for a collaborative approach, in this case the use of a 'learning set' – a small number of people, typically six to eight, who meet on a regular basis to help each other to learn from their experiences and develop new work objectives. The learning set may be made up of colleagues with different roles in an organisation so the idea is to help each other carry out members' own projects rather than develop a shared project together. As an approach in accredited professional learning (for example, MBA programmes) the learning set may be made up of learners from diverse institutions but sharing a common goal of developing each member's professional skills. Many, but not all, forms of action learning, include a coach or advisor who is responsible for promoting learning within the learning set, though he or she will look to hand over this responsibility as the team becomes increasingly self-managing. As with action research, action learning is stimulated by the identification of a real and not easily addressed problem, and like reflective practice in general needs the practitioner to consider a range of options for promoting change and reflecting on outcomes.

STRENGTHS AND WEAKNESSES IN REFLECTIVE PRACTICE APPROACHES

We have seen that there is a diverse tradition of practice research. All share a concern with professional development of those doing the research, not just the outcomes of the research, and at their best they promote the professionalism of practitioners and provide energy and innovation inside an institution. If we are going to improve teaching and learning in any system the engagement of practitioners and their willingness to seek improvement in their own practice is surely key. Thus, few people are in principle against practitioner research whatever form it takes. However, such research, as we have seen already in respect to action research, places demands on practitioners that might be seen as an imposition. Could what has been learnt though reflective practice first hand have been learnt more quickly second hand? Going further, reflective practice is often framed around the idea of empowering the professional but have practitioners asked to be empowered? Finally, some will see all reflective practice as focused on the local. This is not such a problem when you are seeking to develop your practice in an institution in which colleagues are lively, open and offer diverse models of practice from which to learn. However, even with the stimulus of literature and collaborative community, some reflective practitioners are severely limited by the uneven practice and closed thinking that goes on around them.

CASES OF REFLECTIVE PRACTICE

Reflective practice seems core to professional development of teachers and other professionals and indeed a great many have taken part in action research and other practitioner research projects. Accounts of these projects can be found in professional journals, project reports for funding bodies and in a great many dissertations and theses leading to university accredited awards. When it comes to academic journals practitioner reporting is less common. This is not surprising as writing such articles is time consuming and can result in feelings of frustration as reviewers often have a different set of expectations around academic writing than practitioners. However, there are many case studies from academics and practitioners writing together, overviews of interventions, and much practitioner reporting when the practitioner happens to be an academic him or herself. Examples are provided in the following section.

PEER SUPPORT FOR BEREAVED CHILDREN

This first study (Stylianou & Zembylas, 2018) concerns an action research project that had the aim of providing better peer support for bereaved children. It focused on the work that a teacher, Polyxeni, carried out with her class of children aged 10–11 in a

Greek school, and is written by Polyxeni along with a 'critical friend' based at a nearby university. In the project Polyxeni wanted to develop a better way of supporting children in the class when suffering bereavement by getting a more in-depth understanding of children's perspective on loss. The paper begins with an awareness that practice in the area of bereavement is reactive rather than proactive and both children and teachers need to have thought in advance about how to help their peers. In fact, children in her class had many misconceptions about issues of loss and grief or lacked the language to discuss their emotional responses to such issues. Moreover, they did not seem to be able to suggest any ideas on supporting a bereaved peer. Indeed, similar findings are widely reported in the general literature. This led Polyxeni into a collaborative action research project, which she carried out with a critical friend, Michalino.

Her intervention was divided into seven phases, each of which was addressed in one session per week (each session lasted 80 minutes). These interventions covered work on the concept of loss; how emotions can be expressed about loss; appropriate ways of supporting others; expressing empathy; religious traditions and so on. The sessions involved teacher led discussions but also involved more practical learning strategies such as role play and active listening.

The intervention was evaluated via student interview. Children were asked about experiencing a loss, identifying factors that might influence one's grief, providing support to a griever, understanding the role of memories in the grief process, and discussing loss and grief with parents or friends. The interview included flexible follow-up questions to ensure that children were encouraged to add anything that came into their minds. The interviews were conducted by Polyxeni during school time, and due to restrictions of the available time for each interview, the maximum time of an interview was half an hour. In addition, a second critical friend acted as an external observer of both the children's and the teacher's reactions in every lesson.

It was claimed that after the intervention, children were more specific and 'sophisticated' in the ideas they offered for peer support and, in the words of the paper, seemed to take into consideration various factors such as their relationship to the bereaved and the mourner's willingness to accept their support. They also used the new vocabulary of verbal support more carefully, infusing the new knowledge into their stereotypical expressions. They were also able to refer to both active listening and nonverbal communication.

(p. 451)

However, it was noted that as researchers they had not had the opportunity to explore what the children might do in a real life situation.

This is a typical action research project in which the idea of opportunity and problem is merged. The evaluation data support the idea that this project improved classroom practice and helped the young people concerned. The project clearly involved time and effort to say nothing of the commitment needed for reporting to a wider audience. The project involved a collaborative relationship with someone from outside the school and this enabled a wider perspective on change and the evaluation of change.

PRESCHOOL WORK AGAINST BULLYING AND DEGRADING TREATMENT

This second project (Söderström & Löfdahl Hultman, 2017) is described as action learning and it is focused on the professional development of practitioners. Action learning is seen here as learning from experience and reflecting critically on ways in which local problems are addressed.

The paper is not written by the practitioners themselves but by two colleagues, based at a local university, who were leading a project aimed at addressing bullying and 'degrading treatment' in nine Swedish preschools. (Bullying tends to refer to deliberate attempts to cause distress to a child while degrading treatment often feels more personal and is aimed at destabilising a child's dignity.) Such a project would seem to have value at almost any level or in any field of education one can think of. In this case project members attended six sessions at the university and were invited to develop work in their schools. These interventions focused on issues such as collaboration with parents; managing conflict situations; and promoting more tolerant and trusting relationships at the preschool. The interventions were evaluated by teachers in each school and these reports provided the basis for the authors' overall take on the project.

The authors saw the project as successful in helping practitioner in identifying challenges and carrying out changes to address bullying and degrading treatment in schools. However, they found that most of the changes carried out involved heads and teachers, there was very little involvement of the children. This they found disappointing and felt it was a weakness in the project.

Overall the paper shows the value of action learning projects for improving teaching and learning in this case with early years children. One suspects that core to the project was the commitment of the practitioners themselves, the peer support across different institutions and practitioners' access to ideas and help from the local university. However, the authors were keen to draw attention to the tensions in the work as it unfolded as the project coordinators had a goal in mind (the direct involvement of children), which teachers did not pick up on or were not ready to implement. This offers a welcome degree of critical reflection as there is a tendency in some practice learning reporting to offer a kind of 'victory narrative' – we were faced with these problems, which looked insurmountable but look at how well we did. However, such a reflection by the authors opens up questions about ownership and responsibilities in collaborative projects of this kind.

ENVISIONING FUTURES FOR ENVIRONMENTAL AND SUSTAINABILITY EDUCATION

In this action research project (Gardiner, 2017), the author was leading a university module on the theme of *Sustainability and the Future* at the University of Vechta in Germany. This, then, is a case of an academic reflecting on and reporting on their practice.

The content of the module covered an introduction to 'Future Studies methods'. Future Studies looks at likely, and indeed desirable, future scenarios and how and why these scenarios have force. Future Studies tends to draw on different fields of study including sociology, technology and economics, looking back at changes and predicting future trajectories. In this case the course leader, Senan, had a particular focus on issues of sustainability, particularly ecological sustainability.

Senan describes the aim of the course as to develop students' anticipatory competence, which he describes as the competence to engage successfully with the future, manage uncertainty and understand key concepts. He wanted students to engage too with their emotional responses to change and to avoid what he called a 'culture of hopelessness' about the future. For example, he wanted to help students grapple with what their campus and their city might look like in the future and help the students understand developmental trajectories and to feel confident about offering alternatives of their own.

In keeping with this goal, the course was a presented as a collaborative action research project. This meant that students as well as teachers engaged in cycles of reflection or as the author put it a process of: Identify a problem, Think of ways to tackle the problem, Do it, Evaluate it, Modify future practice. The students' reflections were captured in learning diaries.

Problem solving is, as we have seen, key to action research but inevitably perhaps students were facing simulated problems rather than the problems that confronted them in their everyday lives. Indeed, they were often presented with scenarios about the future and asked to comment on how likely these were to unfold. However, Senan maintained a sense of authenticity during the module by having the students work with real data and come back to scenarios located in the local area and indeed in the campus itself. To make the problems come further alive students presented their ideas not only to their colleagues but to a general public. Assessment was a mix of homework activities and an end-of-semester presentation.

Senan's reflection on the project, based on feedback and analysis of learning diaries, was that not only did the course cover the expected knowledge and skills but students also covered a lot of work on emotional responses to change. He hoped that students now felt more confident about their competence to deal with change – as one student put it 'there are things you can really do about it'. A final reflection is that a suitable assessment schema is needed to encourage this kind of participative teaching and learning; it was no good teaching to 'laundry-lists of learning objectives'.

One thing we took away from the study, though not made explicit in the paper, is that if you are committed to action research for your own learning then you should find ways of encouraging your own learners to engage in some kind of action research learning process too. This is not always easy if learners themselves are full-time students – you have to come up with simulated real life problems as here. A second insight from the study is the importance of the emotional dimension to learning – for example Senan wanted his students to feel confident of expressing opinions not just be in receipt of a set of skills and body of knowledge. This makes it difficult to fit an action research learning approach around traditional assessment practice. Such learning needs to be judged on its own terms. The study, like others, leaves open some of the questions about the extent of the co-participation of the students. For example, the teacher is very much in charge of setting the agenda of the course and the assessment. This is not a criticism but simply recognising that, for better or worse, negotiating learning with students can take place across a range of levels.

SUMMARY

We began this book by looking at educational research carried out by practitioners. This is deliberate. Even if practitioners are not enlisted in full blown action research projects, it is their commitment to developing practice that should lie at the heart of any proposal for improving educational practice. The various approaches we have described in this chapter enlist educational research *for teaching and learning* rather than education research *on teaching and learning*. We have seen that action research is about addressing problems through cycles of planning, implementation and evaluation and we gave a picture of the wider idea of reflective practice. All the approaches described in this chapter have the merit of being practice based, frequently collaborative, engaging and motivating for interested teachers and impacting positively on schools. We saw how ideas of reflective practice have become taken up across different contexts and that action learning can itself be an organising principle for teaching and learning. However, we saw tensions in ways of understanding reflective practice and criticisms over the time and skills it needs. We also became aware of the limits on bottom up innovation – there is only so much that can be done. Indeed, we suggested that some schools and teachers might be tempted to apply the more generalisable findings from research rather than work out solutions from, as they see it, scratch. But are there such generalisable findings? This is something we explore in the next chapter.

FURTHER READING

The publishing world is not short of introductory guides to action research and most will assist you in carrying out a project. *You and Your Own Action Research Project* by Jean McNiff (2016) remains a popular introductory guide. Likewise, there are many available introductions to reflective practice and action learning. *Learning by Doing: A guide to teaching and learning methods* by Graham Gibbs (1988) was influential and provides a very straightforward guide for those teaching in higher education. The date of publication suggests it is quite dated but it is not. This book can be downloaded (legally) from Oxford Brookes University eBooks online catalogue. Donald Schön's *The Reflective Practitioner: How professionals think in action* goes back in time too – in this case 1983. However, it remains an accessible and stimulating resource for thinking about professional learning. The criticism made of Schön, as mentioned in this chapter, is what do practitioners do if they do not have access to imaginative ideas for developing their practice in their place of work?

We have introduced some research methods used in educational research in this chapter and there are many books that tend to cover similar ground. *Research Methods in Education* by Louis Cohen, Lawrence Manion and Keith Morrison (2011) is comprehensive. *Introduction to Research Methods in Education* by Keith Punch and Alis Oancea (2014) is balanced and Jerry Wellington's (2015) *Educational Research: Contemporary issues and practical approaches* is both theoretical and practical.

3

GENERALISING ABOUT TEACHING AND LEARNING

INTRODUCTION

In the previous chapter we saw that many practitioners are sceptical of general theories about teaching in their classrooms, preferring to call on their intuition and knowledge of local circumstances. We also saw that such local knowledge can be restrictive and suggested that much can be learnt by accessing relevant resources and working on projects with practitioners from other institutions. However, practice research is always underpinned by a sense that what works in one context will not necessarily transfer to another. Further, nothing in education stands still. What we know today may be overtaken by new insight and the need to address different problems tomorrow.

In this chapter we explore a different path to education research by looking at approaches that offer greater generalisability and, at least to their supporters, greater certainty. Few believe that education research can lead to the construction of general laws that we have in natural science as with, say, the formula $Pt = (4.2 \times L \times T) \div 3,600$, in which Pt is power in kWh; L is litres of water; T the difference in temperature in Celsius, which will precisely calculate the action of heat on water. But perhaps education researchers can follow rigorous enough procedures to state with confidence that one course of action will in most cases be better than another. How can we do this? First, by applying a precise means of assessing the impact of interventions. Second, by accessing data on a large enough scale so that we know we are reporting a general picture not one that is confined to what happened in a single school (or other site of learning). We look at these ideas in this chapter. We begin by looking at experimental methods and randomised control groups, and go on to look at analysis of large data sets including meta-studies, systematic review, PISA and finish with a note on Big Data.

EXPERIMENTAL METHODS: MEASURING WHAT WORKS

An influential behaviorist educator throughout the twentieth century, Edward Thorndike, once claimed that:

> Just as to make the plant grow well the teacher must act in accordance with the laws of botany which concern the growth of plants ... The teacher must act in accordance with the laws of the sciences of human nature.

(Thorndike, 1913/1999: 7)

For Thorndike the sciences of human nature were founded on a simplistic idea of human psychology; what we learnt could be explained in terms of the associations we made between stimulus and response, and ensuring that the right kind of association is made between them. In trying to show this, and in setting out to uncover the science of learning, Thorndike relied on a series of small-scale, often rather trivial experiments (for example guessing the length of a line, remembering a list of words), all undertaken in artificial conditions. Nonetheless he argued his findings were 'convincing and decisive'. Why? The answer lay in his commitment to an experimental method. His experiments involved a comparison between an experimental group (which received an intervention such as the giving of feedback) and a control group without access to the intervention. In these experiments he was interested in what could be objectively measured: there was nothing to be gained from trying to find out about how learning looks from the perspective of the student – it was examining the outcomes of reinforcement strategies that mattered.

This experimental approach to education research has been followed throughout the years and remains popular today. As with Thorndike earlier, some of this work has been undertaken in laboratory style or at least controlled testing. For example, in one study Pressey (1950) looked at early multiple-choice feedback mechanisms. Underlying this interest was anxiety about reinforcement; if students were waiting too long for the results of their tests then, in Pressey's view at least, they would lack positive reinforcement on correct answers and miss out on negative, or better diagnostic, feedback when they had got it wrong. Nowadays feedback can be automatically generated via computer programmes but in 1950, when this paper was published, students were having to work with something more convoluted. They were asked to lay their answer sheet on a card, which contained punched holes to show the correct answers. Using this punched card, they could get positive reinforcement of correct responses and revise incorrect responses until they got the question right. Topics covered Russian vocabulary, technical English vocabulary and the subject matter from two psychology courses.

RUSSIAN VOCABULARY STUDY TEST

Directions: In each line find the English word meaning the same as the Russian word, and punch your pencil into the hole corresponding to that English word. If your pencil goes deep, you are right, and should go on to the next line. But if your pencil barely breaks the paper, you are wrong, and must try again – until you do find the right answer.

ZAPISKA *(a)* plate; *(b)* expensive; *(c)* note; *(d)* bridge.
POTOW *(a)* depth; *(b)* then; *(c)* paper; *(d)* word.

An item from the Russian vocabulary test taken from Pressey (1950)

The findings showed that those taking the test and receiving immediate feedback via the punched card performed, first time round, on a par with those taking the test without feedback. This was as expected. However, the second time round those who had taken the test with punch card feedback outperformed those who had not got immediate feedback. This experiment was conducted on a small scale in classes with 30 or so students in them.

Experimental testing in controlled conditions has some obvious strengths: for example, it really does appear to show what works better (albeit under rather artificial conditions) and even by how much. However, there are obvious problems. Education does not take place in a laboratory. In real life settings students are swayed, in perhaps unpredictable directions, by the novelty of new approaches and teachers may 'contaminate' trials by their implicit enthusiasm, or perhaps disdain, for a course of action or quite simply they may convey their lack of understanding as to what an intervention is trying to achieve. Almost all the early experimental trials, and many later ones, had very short-term goals and were necessarily focused on a narrow range of learning outcomes. Experiments such as the ones conducted by Thorndike and Pressey were also criticised for the trivial nature of the learning involved in that they dealt more with retrieval (recall a list of names) than interpretation (discuss the role of fate in Shakespeare's *Macbeth*). Given that so many teachers spend so much time giving feedback then it is perhaps interesting to know that feedback, even via a punched card in Pressey's experiment earlier, can be useful. However, this is not news and indeed is part of the wisdom of practice. In fact, many of the problems education systems face are not about a lack of good ideas, rather they are about seeing those ideas taken up.

RANDOMISED CONTROLLED TRIALS: A GOLD STANDARD?

The small-scale studies reported here were of their time but policy makers in particular continue to look for more robust evidence of impact to inform their decision-making. This often means undertaking large-scale randomised controlled trials (RCTs) in a style made familiar by medical science. Consider a new treatment for a health problem, for example a drug to treat high blood pressure. If you are put in the position of responsibility for licensing this treatment (or you are a patient advised to follow it) you will want to know if it works. The most obvious way of doing that is to get a sample of patients (those with high blood pressure) and assign them either to a treatment (or experimental) group or to a control group i.e. one that gets a 'placebo' (something that looks the same as the treatment but has no therapeutic value). You can then see if the experimental group has better health outcomes (i.e. blood pressure is reduced) than those without.

To make this a fair trial there should be no bias towards certain types of patient. For example, both groups should have equal proportions of those with personal characteristics such as gender, ethnicity and social group, or particular lifestyles, say those with better diets or who take more exercise. To eliminate such bias the most scientific approach is to randomly assign volunteers to one group or the other. All volunteers (or subjects) are equally likely to be part of one group so that any systematic skewing of the sample should be ironed out. A fair test could also be constructed by using stratified samples, assigning people in proportion to the characteristics of the whole population, but randomisation works better as you might not know in advance what factors are significant in organising your samples. To make matters even more robust, double blind methods are used. This means that patients are not told if they are receiving the treatment or a placebo and neither are those administering the treatment. After the period of time needed to assess the impact of the treatment, researchers can then work out if members of the experimental group experienced better health outcomes than the control group. Researchers can further break down the data and reveal if there are particular kinds of patients for whom the treatment works better than for others. If we trust our lives with RCTs in medicine, should we not do the same in social policy?

In fact, Haynes et al. (2012) say we should trust in RCTs and that these are the 'gold standard' for social policy evaluation. They explain that there are several stages to an RCT including the identification of objectives and suitable measures, drawing conclusions from the findings and adapting policy once we have the results. Adaption is important as like a lot of other researchers in this area they do not see measurement as a goal in itself but a means of informing, not dictating policy. Proponents of RCTs have moved on from the simplistic reasoning that underpinned Thorndike in the last century.

Although interventions can have many goals it seems in education research that almost, by default, learning outcomes are measured. Evaluation might be as straightforward as comparing test scores in group A (the experimental group) with group B (the control group). Findings can be reported using descriptive statistics, for example researchers can calculate mean test scores pre- and post-intervention and can further break scores down by age range, gender, ethnicity or other criteria. At a more sophisticated level, researchers may employ inferential statistics to assess the strength of the relationship between intervention and outcome – here an association is reported as significant if it carries a p-value of less than 0.05. The principle is that in a p-value of less than 0.05 a reported association is overwhelmingly likely to be meaningful and only in 5 per cent of cases would it be a matter of chance (a probability of 0.05). It is important to note here that a significant relationship is not proof that variable X *causes* outcome Y, only that the two appear to be associated. Further, failure to establish statistical significance does not mean the relationship is insignificant in the ordinary use of the word.

Statistical tests could be run on subgroup data too. For example, you might be particularly interested in how a policy, say introducing breakfast clubs into schools, affects children from poorer families. This means that an intervention that shows relatively little overall impact might still be effective if it works particularly well for the group you are targeting, for example those who belong to an at-risk group. Armed with knowledge of impact, policy makers could decide to 'roll out' an intervention more generally and indeed more RCTs could be set up to evaluate the best ways of doing this. The strength of the RCT is that it offers a comparison between people in similar circumstances. It is not asking what you think should work but provides what looks like objective evidence of what does work. RCTs are time consuming and need to be carefully designed but they do not have to involve massive numbers of participants nor be hugely expensive to construct, even if the interventions themselves can be.

There are then many strengths to RCTs in education and if conducted on a larger scale they offer increased reliability certainly if compared against small-scale studies of the last century. However,

RCTs generate a number of concerns – as seen for example in Biesta (2010) and Silberman (2002). First, RCTs, especially when set up to influence government policy, are rarely given the time needed to show long term effect – in fact, the example reported later (Banerjee et al., 2007) was unusual in looking at learning gains over two years. This was useful as it identified some scaling back of impact over time, which is what you would expect to happen. Second, RCTs often end up measuring what can be measured easily and objectively rather than what is important. In fact, the temptation is to measure cognitive gains as students are tested as a matter of course in school and past test scores are often stored and made accessible to researchers. For example, in our earlier case, breakfast club interventions are often assessed by impact on test outcomes but perhaps such an intervention should be assessed for its possible contribution to student health, well-being and feelings of belonging, all much more difficult to measure (Defeyter et al., 2010). Third, RCTs create ethical problems. If the intervention is an early success then would it be fair to continue to exclude control groups from accessing it? And if the intervention looks unsuccessful why should students be expected to continue with it? Fourth, the analogy of the placebo in medical trials is misleading when discussing education. The control group is not simply missing out on an intervention, they are receiving a different kind of intervention, which often turns out to be a patently inferior one. This is stacking the odds in favour of the intervention.

RCTs are valuable tools but they are not a 'gold standard' as often claimed. Instead they are part of the mix in deciding how to improve educational systems. They offer credible evidence of impact but they can often lack a sophisticated understanding of why interventions work (or do not work) and can miss the wider picture. As a final qualification RCTs are sometimes the first point of call for those commissioning educational research but this is wrong; RCTs are designed to *test* interventions not generate possibilities. Here the medical analogy is helpful. New treatments are tested in large-scale trials but they are developed by small-scale experiment and discussion among professional researchers. Sometimes, as famously illustrated in the identification of penicillin, they happen by accident. We look next at two examples of RCT studies.

REMEDYING EDUCATION: EVIDENCE FROM TWO RANDOMISED
EXPERIMENTS IN INDIA

This trial (Banerjee et al., 2007), referred to in Haynes et al. (2012), concerns a remedial education programme in India to address underachievement among young learners. Two interventions are discussed and we look at the first of these, which involved employing a mentor/learning support worker (a young woman, recruited from the local community, who had herself finished secondary school) to enable children to access remedial support for basic skills. This did not involve extra hours of teaching. Rather, the children were taken out of the regular classroom for two hours per day (the school day was about four hours) to work in small groups in any available space inside the school. Using an RCT approach, the researchers compared outcomes from those receiving this support to those attending their regular classroom for the full four hours instead. End of term tests suggested that those receiving the support demonstrated large learning gains, which were sustained over time (though with some reversion). The study involved large numbers of students, for example 5,264 from 49 schools in the experimental group in Year 1.

Many randomised control trials are criticised for not costing the interventions they introduce. Here no precise costing for rolling out this intervention were given but the authors emphasise that this programme was cost effective and scalable. The small group support was provided by women who were trained for a short period of time and paid very modestly on local rates (around 10–15 US dollars, per month).

An interesting feature of this study is that although RCTs focus on what can be measured, and often avoid too much conjecture for the reasons why certain outcomes materialised, the authors suggest that the poor performance of students in the control group may have come about because teachers were having to work towards a prescribed curriculum, and felt unable to go back to help students once they had fallen behind. Indeed, in the words of the paper, normal classroom teaching may end up 'being completely ineffective' for those who are failing to keep up. Second, it is suggested that it was very helpful that students in the experimental group shared a common background with their support teachers. In contrast their regular classroom teachers may be dismissive of these children's needs, feeling they were doing a 'favour by teaching children from erstwhile "untouchable" communities or very poor migrants'. These conjectures are really helpful but they show a problem in the methodology of RCT mentioned earlier. For it might not be that the intervention itself was particularly effective but what was happening in the control group was particularly ineffective.

THE EFFECT OF A TRAINING PROGRAMME ON SCHOOL NURSES' KNOWLEDGE, ATTITUDES AND DEPRESSION RECOGNITION SKILLS

Our second study (Haddad et al., 2018) concerns a programme to support school nurses in England. The study was triggered by growing questions asked about the mental health of young people and a recognition that school nurses play a vital role in identifying and managing mental health problems. Hence a training programme was designed to assist nurses in this case by improving their knowledge, attitudes and recognition skills for depression.

One hundred and forty-six school nurses from thirteen Primary Care Trusts (PCTs) in London were randomly allocated to an experimental or control group. (In this case the control group would receive the training programme but at a later time.) A programme of online and face-to-face training was devised and the impact was measured at the start of the programme and three months and nine months into the training. The programme was reported as successful. Training was associated with significant improvements in some areas of the nurses' working including the ability to make more specific judgements about depression; improved knowledge about depression and greater confidence in handling their professional role.

One thing missing from the paper was the cost of the programme. Health professionals were asked to contribute to the design of the programme so as to access 'up to date best practice' and there was input from nurses in order to frame the programme in an accessible manner. The delivery of the programme involved face-to-face teaching as well as online resources. This sounds quite labour intensive and carried a cost. Unlike the Banerjee et al. study discussed earlier there is less conjecture on why the programme was successful, but it seems fair to conclude that if you provide a well-resourced programme and offer it to interested health professionals then you should notice learning gains, though such gains should never be taken for granted. However, it is not clear if this particular programme is the only way to address these training needs; other approaches might work and some may be more cost effective.

META-STUDIES

Even the most extensive RCTs are limited in size and scope. One way of expanding the reach of your analysis is to carry out a meta-analysis that combines the results of multiple experimental studies. Imagine, for example, that you think providing more homework for your students will result in better learning outcomes. You can of course set up a small trial to test this, giving more homework to the experimental group and keeping a control group that follows existing practice. At the end of the trial perhaps you find a small but not negligible impact on test scores. However, you still face the problem of the small-scale nature of the study and there is little here to convince policy makers or even the school leaders that giving more homework 'works'. It would be so much better if we could supplement this one intervention by looking at all the experimental studies on homework that had ever been done, and arrive at a general picture arising from these studies, before starting out on our intervention (see, for example, Fan et al.'s 2017 review of homework in maths and science). This aggregation of studies is a meta-review.

Of course, in carrying out a meta-review the immediate question is which studies to access and how to access them. Researchers generally begin by deciding on key words so that relevant studies can be identified and selecting journals that meet certain quality criteria. A strength of a meta-analysis is that the selection and analysis of papers is undertaken using what appear as objective criteria, so that you are not prejudging which papers are relevant and which are not. However, selection of studies is rarely straight-forward. For example, key words need to be refined as their meaning may change according to time and place. For example, *collaborative* and *cooperative* are well-used terms in education with the idea that collaborative learning involves working together to create joint products, while cooperative learning involves individuals working on specific parts of a problem so that each member of a group makes a contribution. In the latter there is not the same deep level of sharing as expected in collaborative approaches. However, as it happens, the terms collaborative and cooperative have been used in reverse so that the former involves sharing out the work and the latter a more integrated approach. Thus, if you use the key word 'collaborative' you might get papers that are not collaborative at all in the sense you mean and miss others that are collaborative but not described as such. This points to the importance of having an in-depth understanding of the topic being researched.

Once having defined the papers the findings can be identified, aggregated and weighted, i.e. larger sample sizes count more. We can then give a measure of learning gain. Here many researchers use the concept of effect size (Higgins, 2018). Effect size is defined as the 'standardised mean difference' between experimental and control groups. So that if the effect size is large (say 0.8) this means that the mean performer in the experimental group will now be performing at a higher level, one on par with the top performers in the control group. Conversely with low effect size the mean performer in the experimental group will not have shifted much in relation to the control group.

Clearly the meta-analysis approach is only as good as the studies themselves and while researchers can introduce quality criteria in the selection of the studies to weed out dubious ones, there are question marks over the representativeness of the literature in the first place. For example, there are economic and cultural considerations, which may bias the literature to research taking place in the English speaking, economically developed world and exclude research in developing countries. It has often been assumed too that there is a general bias towards positive rather than 'no evidence of impact' studies. Perhaps this reflects a preference on the part of reviewers and editors to publish the more arresting studies: after all who wants to read about what did not happen? Or it might simply be that academics are more willing to put time and effort into publishing positive findings. Whatever the case we can end up with an over optimistic view of an intervention and an assumption of generalisability that is misplaced.

HATTIE AND VISIBLE TEACHING

A very well reported study is that of Hattie (2013) who carried out a meta-analysis of the effectiveness of a range of variables on student achievement. These variables, 138 in total, covered a range of student, home, school, teacher, curricula and teaching issues (for example class sizes, collaborative approaches to learning, feedback, ability grouping and so on). This was a huge undertaking and took in 800 meta-analysis studies (this meant that Hattie's study was in part a meta meta-analysis) and over 50,000 smaller studies that had taken placed over 15 years. The sheer scope and size of Hattie's work gave it a credibility, which policy makers at least have found very convincing; its influence has surprised Hattie himself (Hanna, 2017).

Rather than find out what works and what does not work, Hattie was interested in the question of what works better. To do this he calculated the weighted effect size for all the 138 factors in which he was interested and created categories of large effect size (what seemed to have desired effects), mid effect size (less desired effects) and so on. Perhaps it is not surprising that some factors, such as giving feedback, turned out to be very effective but some that might have been assumed to be effective in his study (e.g. class sizes) turned out to be less effective than many thought. Based on these effect sizes he was able to present a vision of education based upon the idea of an 'activator teacher', someone who practised what he called 'visible teaching'. He argued that,

> Visible teaching and learning occurs when learning is the explicit goal, when it is appropriately challenging, when the teacher and student both seek to ascertain whether and to what degree the challenging goal is attained, when there is deliberate practice aimed at attaining mastery of the goal, when there is feedback given and sought, and when there are active, passionate and engaging people participating in the act of learning.
>
> (Hattie, 2013: 22)

Visible teaching is contrasted to more exploratory ideas of learning or at least ones in which learners are expected to alight upon learning outcomes for themselves.

This idea of visible teaching is interesting as meta-analyses are often criticised for letting the data speak for themselves. Hattie in contrast is theorising about teaching and learning by drawing on the data to present an ideal type of teaching. While this theorisation is reasonable and helpful it is worth stressing that it is an interpretation; visible teaching is speculative while reporting effect sizes is 'objective'. This is important as Hattie's visible teaching is often presented by school leaders and by policy makers as, if not infallible, at least as carrying an authority well above many other studies. This is wrong. Visible teaching is a well-argued interpretation of data but it is conjecture: well grounded conjecture, but conjecture. Other people could use the same data and reach different conclusions. For that matter other researchers could set up the frame for selection differently and make different decisions as to what to include. Finally, a strength in Hattie is that it considered studies that took place over a long period of time – meta-studies always look back. But what might have been a less effective approach might now be more effective once teachers and students get used to it and, further, what is available to students today is very different in terms of technology (Fullan & Langworthy, 2013).

SYSTEMATIC REVIEWS AND BEING SYSTEMATIC

Meta-reviews can be seen as a particular focused kind of literature review – one that draws conclusions from experimental studies. However, it is also possible to aggregate studies in more flexible ways, as a literature review. A literature review gives an overview of a particular field or topic. It covers what has been said, who has said it, and sets out prevailing theories and methodologies and as such may be a prelude to a case study or other one-off study, as we discuss in our next chapter. In terms of generalising from past studies, of particular interest for this chapter is the systematic literature review, which, like meta-analyses, uses explicit predetermined criteria for deciding which studies to include and closely defined protocols for analysis and reporting. Indeed, a meta-analysis could be considered a type of systematic review. However, some systematic reviews are more flexible than meta-analyses and may try to incorporate a broader range of approaches by including case studies and other more 'qualitative' approaches. One particularly important example of a flexible systematic review was carried out over 20 years ago into assessment practices, strategies and theories. This was work by Black and Wiliam and is sometimes called their 'black box' research (e.g. Black & Wiliam 1998). As well as having a great deal of practical application in the classroom, the research also influenced and informed policy on assessment in many educational systems in the twenty-first century (not a small accomplishment). The term 'assessment for learning' (AfL) has now become commonplace and has led to a new attitude to teachers' assessment practices. The 'black box' study has further led to a wealth of terms now commonly used in schools and higher education, such as summative assessment, formative and diagnostic assessment, all more or less under the umbrella of AfL.

It is worth noting that although Black and Wiliam's systematic review work was commissioned by the Assessment Reform Group, a working group of educational researchers, they were not bound by rigid criteria setting out which studies could be included and which could not. Instead, the group provided a practical definition of AfL by describing 'assessment that promotes learning' in various ways such as assessment that shares learning goals with students; involves students in self-assessment; provides feedback so that students know the next steps they need to take; involves teachers and students reviewing and reflecting on assessment results together. This shows that a systematic review does not have to follow certain 'objective' selection criteria in order to be productive and have an impact. It also shows the value of treating systematic review as an inquiry into practice, carried out by those with access to practice knowledge, rather than a technical exercise.

ANALYSIS OF LARGE DATA SETS

An alternative approach to generalising is not so much to draw on past findings but to use archives of data and retrospectively analyse them (this is often called secondary data analysis and by some a kind of post hoc analysis). For example, to go back to breakfast clubs, rather than setting up a new intervention around breakfast clubs we could work backwards. We could identify sites in which breakfast clubs had been introduced and compare students in these sites with students, with similar characteristics, in schools without access to breakfast clubs. This would involve many practical issues but in principle such an approach offers three key advantages. First, the data are already there. There is no need to construct expensive and time-consuming interventions. Second, in contrast to meta-analyses geared around the impact of interventions we are looking at naturally occurring developments and this provides greater ecological validity, i.e. findings that take the context of an intervention into account. Third, the research can include breakfast clubs that have been running over a period of years rather than ones set up in the lifespan of a policy. This provides a longitudinal perspective that RCTs often lack.

There are, however, some criticisms of retrospective testing. First, you are working with the data already provided and you may be missing some really important data that schools do not routinely keep. You are also unlikely to be aware of the circumstances under which the data were collected and may skip asking critical questions about their reliability. Second, to the purist statistician, secondary data analysis can encourage a trawling through of data and seeing what comes up. This is disturbing as it is more likely to result in so-called spurious explanation (explanation based on the random association between variables) as you have not had to do the hard graft in setting out the basis for a hypothesis in the first place.

There are some very large data sets, particularly on student achievement, for those interested in large-scale secondary data analysis. For example, in England there is a particularly useful data set – the National Pupil Database (NPD) – which contains data on all those in public education in some cases from the ages of 2–21. Personal and school characteristics can be linked to data on student attainment and exam results. The NPD contains data on over 20 million students. It can be accessed by researchers, with appropriate safeguards, and has often been used in studies of achievement both to consider the national picture but also in more local studies as the following.

SCHOOL EFFECTS AND ETHNIC, GENDER AND SOCIOECONOMIC GAPS IN EDUCATIONAL ACHIEVEMENT AT AGE 11

This study (Strand, 2014) looked at 2,836 11-year-olds and their national test results in English, mathematics and science. This took place in one ethnically diverse inner London borough, enabling the author to explore the influence of socioeconomic status (SES), ethnicity and gender on attainment. Thus, here SES ethnicity and gender are independent variables (the things expected to create an effect) and attainment the dependent variable (the thing that is affected). Test results were compared at ages 7 and 11 so this study was looking at learning gain over a four-year period and what influenced it. To do this each variable needed to be defined and this was done in the following ways:

Socioeconomic status (SES) was primarily measured first by entitlement to free school meals – this is often used in research in the UK to indicate whether the student comes from a family in receipt of state benefits.

Ethnic group: each student's ethnic group was recorded in one of 18 categories as used in the national school census but these were later amalgamated to create larger categories.

Age 7 test score: these were results of national tests in reading, writing, and mathematics at the end of Year 2 when aged around 7 years. The average score across all three tests was calculated.

Gender: was recorded as boy/girl.

Other variables were age within year group (this plays an important role in achievement as there can be nearly a year's difference in age between oldest and youngest); special education needs as recorded; student mobility i.e. how long students had been at the school; absence; English as an additional language.

In brief, the findings of the study showed that the groups with the lowest educational achievement and poorest progress were Black Caribbean and White British low SES students. Girls on average achieved significantly higher scores than boys, and students from some ethnic groups scored significantly higher than White British students. Progress seems to be affected, in order, by SES and ethnicity, but gender far less. Schools did make a difference to achievement in that children with similar characteristics did achieve more in some schools than others but if school effects were large, they were also uneven.

This kind of study gives useful insight into what affects achievement and is one of several in the UK that has drawn attention to the varying impact of ethnicity (i.e. some ethnic groups do very well regardless of SES) and the recurring underachievement of white working class students, in particular white working class boys, and black Caribbean boys. It is difficult to see how these subtleties would be picked up without large-scale studies. However, such studies need to be complemented by others that show how, say, SES works and why the effect of disadvantage seem so hard to shift.

THE PROGRAMME FOR INTERNATIONAL STUDENT ASSESSMENT (PISA)

Discussion of the use of large sets of data leads naturally onto the role of PISA carried out on behalf of the Organisation for Economic Co-operation and Development (OECD). PISA provide tests every three years in mathematics, science, and reading, and more recently collaborative problem solving. The aim is to compare educational outcomes across countries (Sellar et al., 2017).

The tests are given to representative samples of 15-year-olds (by the time the tests are taken some students have just passed 16) and involve a mix of multiple-choice and longer answers, as well as some more innovative testing of collaborative learning. Tests are quite lengthy and students do need not to take all of them. Participating students also answer a questionnaire on their background, including learning habits, motivation and family, while school directors fill in a questionnaire describing school demographics, funding and indicate their concerns about teaching and learning. The testing has been going since 2000 and has increased in profile over time. In 2015 over half a million students, representing 28 million 15-year-olds in 72 countries and economies took part.

PISA results are reported by OECD in a variety of formats including accessible overviews, country-by-country profiles and more detailed technical accounts. One aim of the exercise is to provide a snapshot of how education systems are doing both over time and against each other. However, by comparing test outcomes against characteristics such as access; school autonomy; parental involvement; funding and so on, PISA researchers are able to speculate on the impact of a number of variables on attainment. Findings are broken down in useful ways, for example by gender, migrant students, teacher student ratios, expenditure (as a percentage of national income), length of school year, status and composition of the teaching profession and so on.

The findings offered by PISA are difficult to summarise as so much is covered. However, it is clear from PISA that student knowledge and skills in the areas that are being tested do vary from system to system and the background data seem to show the importance of school climate and support for teacher professional development. The findings show the continuing influence of SES but also the ways that a culture of 'resilience' can help students overcome disadvantage. Spending on training teachers and on their continuing professional development comes over as important and could be prioritised over reducing class sizes. There were some achievement gaps in outcomes between girls and boys (though not a consistent picture) but a more persistent gap between migrant and indigenous children. Worldwide, the issues that schools face seem to include truancy, drugs, bullying behaviour and teacher resistance to change. When choosing a school for their child, parents are likely to consider a safe school environment as more important than their child's academic achievement at the school.

The range of data is vast and large sums have been spent in designing 'fair and rigorous' tests. OECD modelling of findings is sophisticated and for many policy makers PISA looks like objective evidence of educational outcome. Unfortunately, PISA has in many countries been kicked around as a political football. Policy makers, not just instinctive conservatives, have been much struck by the success of East Asian students in these tests. This had led to the use of the findings to support the argument that what works is the direct instructional teaching that is seen as a feature of East Asian educational systems and to some extent this idea seems to triangulate with Hattie's idea of visible learning, described earlier, at least in the mind of many policy makers. In contrast those looking to modernise or change the curriculum have often been put on the defensive. They have criticised the reliability of the tests, the capacity for 'game playing' within educational systems (for example 'teaching to the test', making sure some weaker students do not take the test, providing practice tests in advance) as well as the exclusion of those suspended from or unable to access school. They also criticise, and this has become a recurring theme of the studies in this chapter, the bias towards traditional subjects and neglect of arts and social science. Some commentators too have latched on to the success of Finland in these tests as an example of a system that gives high status to teachers, supports teachers' professional learning and offers a kinder pedagogy (Sahlberg, 2011). Others have noted the pressure in East Asian systems for a more creative and less stress filled curriculum.

OECD tends to be quite cautious in describing what they have found, for example, the OECD does not combine scores from the different tests to give an overall rank order for education systems. Policy makers and press reporting tends to be much cruder and there is much 'over-interpretation' of findings. In fact, the findings are so varied that it would be a poor politician who could not find something in support of the changes they have introduced, or want to introduce. One disturbing development has been to use PISA tests as a guide for curriculum change, and general education reform – this is discussed in the case of Spain by Choi and Jerrim (2016), but it is becoming a global phenomenon. PISA led policy making will, at its worst, lead to further game playing, a search for short-term fixes to improve results rather than longer term work on changing the culture of schools and status of teachers. There is, then, a role here for education researchers to promote critical and responsible use of PISA data. For example, PISA data can be used to carry out further secondary data analysis. For example, Fuchs and Wößmann (2008) use the data to model the variables that affect learning outcomes and Hanushek and Woßmann (2010) explore the economic consequences of education. The latter paper shows that education plays a vital economic role by allowing the creativity and transferable skills needed for innovation to develop across a population, albeit it is the quality of education that counts, not education in itself. As the authors put it, 'What people know matters'. PISA findings can, further, spur new thinking about issues such as vocational routes to education and school autonomy. Global testing can provide the impetus for a new phase of critical comparative studies that compare cultures and education systems in imaginative ways. An example here is Jerrim (2015) who looks at children from East Asian backgrounds who have been schooled in Australia. He finds similar levels of high achievement as often found among East Asian children schooled in East Asian systems. The study points to the importance of family, and a culture of resilience within the family, rather than the existence of a particularly effective East Asian system of schooling.

BIG DATA

In looking at the use of large data sets, we have so far considered data that have been collected for specific purposes and then analysed with particular goals in mind. A new approach to data management has been presented by Big Data. Definitions of Big Data centre on the three Vs: volume, variety and velocity. In other words, we have more data (volume), more kinds of data (variety) and data that can be more quickly assembled and indeed continually updated (velocity). Data are so plentiful as so much has been collected with no clear purpose in mind – for example tech companies set up systems to track many different kinds of user activity without knowing at the outset what they are doing it for. However, Big Data can find useful applications. For example, data on traffic flow are constantly accessed and updated in order to manage control measures such as traffic lights; Twitter feeds can be processed to identify how virus and other infections spread through a population; environmental hazards can be reported through the use of sensors. On the other hand, the way that data have been collected automatically and without permission, and the misuse of data have been the subject of growing concerns, for example, data generated via Facebook has been used to manipulate consumer behaviour and indeed political activity.

Big Data are collected as a matter of course in many educational systems and allow the generation of powerful models, which assist decision-making at policy, institution and teacher levels (see Williamson, 2017). Often these models are in the form of so-called dashboards allowing those with access to see students' activity (for example attendance at lectures, visits to the library, meetings with tutors, participation in virtual learning), all of which is automatically recorded. These dashboards can be used to call up data on individuals, but also groups (for example to compare participation between students from high or low SES backgrounds). The value here is that you can compare activity profiles of individuals with wider groups. Systems can also generate ideal profiles based on past data. For example, the high achieving student may, predictably, turn out to be someone who is actively involved in virtual learning and who attends the library frequently, though the profile may have less predictable elements too, say, participation in social activities. Algorithms can be designed that alert students and tutors to dips in activity (for example missing online assessments) with the idea that such alerts can be offered 'just in time' rather than when it is too late (Sclater et al., 2016).

A more ambitious use of data is to draw on profiles of past learners to tailor learning to individuals within online individualised programmes. For example, several commercial companies offer Adaptive Learning Platforms, which offer what they call algorithmic assessment. This is meant to enable online learning systems to personalise activities to each student's preferences and background skills, for example stronger students can avoid activities that are not challenging enough. This kind of approach has come under attack for promoting an independent learning approach, when it is far from clear that such an approach is appropriate or indeed effective, and for deskilling the teacher. Indeed, teachers do a lot of 'real time' assessment of their classes in that they get a feel for their students, and how they best learn, and adapt their teaching accordingly. As we see in the next chapter, this can be very effective but it is difficult to log or describe.

Overall, then, Big Data can be very helpful to educational institutions and to the staff that work in them. Big Data presents many opportunities for educational researchers in accessing what goes on rather than what people say goes on. There are some important provisos. First, the focus is always on what can be measured digitally; this can mean missing out on other important forms of monitoring. Second, learning analytics might lead us into particular directions unthinkingly and without critical scrutiny – for example Kwet (2017) criticises an emerging national e-education system in South Africa for a lack of transparency and for undermining teacher professionalism. Third, there is a danger in over generalisation. For example, suppose we know that in general that those who take part in online discussion tend to achieve higher learning outcomes, this does not mean that such participation will lead to such outcomes or that failure to participate will lead to under-achievement. Data processing only gives us patterns, not certainties. Finally, there is a question of ethics: what is it appropriate to collect, who has access to it, and what is it used for? It is worth noting here that a lot more data could be collected on all students, or for that matter staff, simply by downloading activity stored on mobile phones. This could tell us time and extent of participation in social network sites, logs of physical movements throughout the day, online interactions with peers and teachers, patterns of sleep and other routines and so on. However, few would find such downloading of data to be acceptable.

SUMMARY

In this chapter we have looked at attempts to generalise about education. There are common strengths to many of these approaches; in particular they enable a comparison of intervention against non-intervention and provide a level of credibility that both policy makers and indeed the wider public find convincing. At their best, they are underpinned by knowledge of the field and provide reasoned explanation of why something works. Supporters of these approaches do not see them as ends in themselves but as ways of triggering developments in education systems.

However, we have also argued that claims to scientific certainty are untenable. Behaviourist experiments in the past were artificially constructed, and some of the work was trivial. RCTs leave questions as to non-intervention treatment and neglect explanation. Meta-analyses are more convincing, but can be skewed by what is

GENERALISING ABOUT TEACHING AND LEARNING

publically available. We have also seen that a common issue in many attempts to generalise is that they are measuring what can be or what is routinely measured. This has at times distorted research by over-focusing on test scores in literacy, maths and science. Reporting of studies is further skewed by policy makers and the press, particularly in the case of PISA.

All the work we have described in this chapter contributes to the wider picture of educational research. Our criticism is that these studies based on 'what works' are often seen as a 'gold standard' rather than one approach among many.

FURTHER READING

The theme of this chapter is whether we can make generalisations about education and this has raised questions about whether there is a science of education research. In general, education researchers, including many who are quite happy working within quantitative fields, are not very taken with the idea of education as a science. A historical take on education research is offered in Ellen Lagemann's (2002)'s *An Elusive Science: The troubling history of education research*, this gives a long view albeit weighted towards the USA.

For more on RCTs look at the brief overview by Laura Haynes and colleagues (2012) *Test, Learn, Adapt: Developing public policy with randomised controlled trials*. This is a report designed for UK government but has wider value. Like others, the authors are at their most convincing when they say that RCT's do not provide the solutions for policy but help in the process; they are least convincing when 'banging the drum' for RCTs. The report is available online at www.gov.uk/government/publications/test-learn-adapt-developing-public-policy-with-randomised-controlled-trials.

For more on meta-analysis see Steve Higgins's (2018) *Improving Learning: Meta-analysis of intervention research in education*. Higgins gives a good overview of the pro and cons of meta-analysis and an introduction to statistical methods along the way. He sees meta-analyses as one link in an approach to developing educational practice, offering a balanced and accessible commentary.

For systematic review, at least for a purist approach, you might try Carole Torgerson's (2003) *Systematic Reviews*. There is a useful resource on systematic review offered by the EPPI Centre – a 'specialist centre for: (i) developing methods for systematic reviewing and synthesis of research evidence; and (ii) developing methods for the study of the use research'. Go to https://eppi.ioe.ac.uk/.

We have not cited individual PISA reports, simply go to the PISA website to access reports, details of methodology and an interactive map with results for each educational system. The site is continually updated: www.oecd.org/pisa/.

Sam Sellar et al.'s (2017) *The Global Education Race: Taking the measure of PISA and international testing* gives a useful background to PISA with criticism as to how PISA is being interpreted.

Big Data is a new field for education research and some of the background, applications and arguments are discussed in Ben Williamson's (2017) *Big Data in Education: The digital future of learning, policy and practice*. He argues ethical issues need to be central to future research and practice.

4

DESCRIBING AND CATEGORISING IN EDUCATION RESEARCH

INTRODUCTION

In the previous chapter we saw that by searching for generalisations about teaching and learning researchers help us understand how factors such as student background, teaching culture and organisation of schools are related to educational outcomes as measured by national and international tests. However, research in this tradition can be criticised for being too general and reaching for blanket statements about this or that strategy, or policy, without looking too closely at details. One consequence is that we often read a lot about the association of variables but less on *why* variables should be related to certain outcomes, and indeed why we should assume outcomes can be broken down into predictable patterns of cause and effect in the first place. Other types of research are needed to dig beneath the surface and to offer more nuanced ways of describing and explaining teaching and learning. In this chapter we see how important it is for researchers to categorise what they see if they want to compare classes and go on to offer useful advice for practitioners and policy makers. The chapter begins with a background to categorising and moves into examples of research that have involved classroom room talk: first, teacher questioning, then children talking together. We look next at education leadership and present a case study of leadership in Vietnam. We finish with a note on the wisdom of teaching.

CATEGORIES AND CATEGORISING

Education researchers need a nuanced language to describe the different types of actions, movements and talk that go on in teaching and learning and in this chapter we begin by looking at a typical lesson. In the scenario we put aside contextual details such as how many students there are, the age group of the students and their gender and focus instead on what a teacher is doing when teaching a class. Is there more going on than first meets the eye?

AN EVERYDAY LESSON

Before the lesson, the teacher watches as the children enter the room. Without the students being aware of it she is judging their mood – are they overexcited after playing outside? Are they bored or tired as they look forward to their lunch? She checks that they sit down according to her seating plan. At the start of the lesson she signals for the students to settle. They are slow to do so. She counts down 5, 4, 3, 2, and she gets their attention.

Her lesson is one of a series on weather patterns. In recent lessons she has covered some of the features of meteorological maps and how rain and snow forms. Today she is explaining wind movement. She wants her students to understand that wind is the movement of denser air into the space left by lighter air. She knows this is quite difficult and abstract for her students to grasp so she introduces key terms carefully and questions them about their understanding: What intense wind movement have you seen? When did you see these? What do we call it when we have very strong winds? Does wind consist of anything? She encourages participation from the students. She knows too that some students will find the words 'wind movement' hilarious as it will conjure up the idea of passing wind, so she makes a joke about this and ask the class to move on and think about weather instead.

She explains that wind is the movement of large amounts of air and in fact we can think of wind as a gas that flows around the surface of the earth. But why does wind flow? She recaps a recent lesson on air pressure and explains that wind is the movement of air from an area of high pressure towards one of low pressure. High winds are caused when air moves between areas with large differences in air pressure. She illustrates the point by holding up a balloon. She blows up the balloon and asks 'what will happen as I let go?' The class all know that the balloon will take off, she lets go and indeed the balloon whirls around the room. She asks for explanations as to what has happened. The children talk about the balloon being pushed, the balloon deflating, the pressure being exerted on the balloon. These are all common sense explanations, but she explains that what is happening is that the air pressure inside the balloon must rebalance with the air pressure around it. Wind is the movement of denser air, the air under high pressure, into the space left by lighter air. She explains this is what is happening when we get windy days. She goes on to explain how high and low pressures are marked on maps and what causes hot and cold air in the first place. She then provides short film clips to illustrate examples of intense wind movements and explains how wind speeds are measured. She explains that everyday words such as breeze, gale, hurricane, all words with which the students are familiar, have precise meanings when reporting wind speeds. She looks round the room to check understanding and asks questions to refocus the attention of some of the students who appear to be losing interest – 'Jools, what did I just say?', 'Sanjiv, how is air pressure represented on a map?'. Some of her questions are more conceptual and are aimed at the whole class (e.g. 'Can anyone tell me about the wind speed if the isobars on a weather map were quite far apart?').

There is a clock on the wall and she glances at it every now and then to see if she is on track – she must rein in her talking and give the children some tasks to do. They need time to think about what they have covered and an opportunity to practise their weather skills. She passes round a printed resource and gets them working on short scenarios in which they have to interpret meteorological data and describe the likely weather outcomes. They are encouraged to share ideas. She circulates the room, checking the children are attempting the tasks and providing help to those who are floundering. She glances again at the clock and finishes the lesson with a recap of key points with more questions asked. She asks them to watch/read or listen to weather forecasts at home and report back on what they found out in the next lesson. She has the children leave quietly to go onto their next lesson.

We have seen lessons like these countless times, often they do not run as smoothly as described here and many lack the novelty this teacher introduced with her whirling balloon but the way the lesson is designed is quite familiar: the teacher is explaining something and the students are practising what they have learnt. But is that all we can say?

Well no. Education researchers want to pick beneath the surface and try to explain what is going on. For example, there is a shape to the lesson, which we can break down in more detail into episodes, say episodes of *settling, explaining, handing over to students* and *recap*. What percentage of time in each lesson is given to these phases? Is there anything we can say about what happens when a teacher spends more time on one phase than usual? In fact, the teacher in our example has an informal understanding of how long she can talk for, but do all teachers have this sense, and where does it come from?

Then there is a lot of classroom management going on. The teacher watches the students enter the room and she picks up on language (wind movement) that might be the cause of disruption. She monitors and intervenes while students are working and she uses tasks not only to support children's learning but to manage the lesson. She appears to do all this quietly and efficiently but is that normal? By watching classrooms like these education researchers can identify the different facets of classroom management, naming and illustrating the importance of strategies such as *monitoring; circulating; showing presence; managing time;* and *task setting*. More generally we can see the teacher is *being proactive*, for example, she circulates the class, picking up difficulties, not waiting for them to appear; she encourages students *to be positive* and involved. Once we have an idea of the strategies that teachers use, we can then compare to other classrooms – perhaps ones that are not running so smoothly – and think about why they differ. This might lead on to the kind of work on generalisation that we saw last chapter, and a quick search will call up many examples of meta-analyses of classroom management (e.g. Korpershoek et al., 2016 looking at primary school classrooms) but no kind of generalisation would be possible without the detailed and often painstaking examination of case study lessons.

If this work of categorising and explaining classroom management sounds straightforward, it is not. Classrooms are difficult to research as expectations about teaching and learning are cemented over time in ways that those involved may find difficult to recall or explain to themselves, let alone to another person. In our scenario the teacher counted backwards in order to establish quiet and attention. This clearly had something to do with rules and sanctions but we would need to ask her to find out more. Perhaps the teacher once explained there were sanctions if students carried on speaking after she had finished counting backwards or perhaps this rule is just something known about the teacher and passed down from one class to another. Perhaps it was a rule that was discussed with students and they themselves suggested (see Hollingshead et al., 2016). The rule does not need to be continually repeated but everyone knows it is there. Students bring their understanding of the context into school and a great deal of what goes on in the classroom cannot be explained solely in terms of strategies teachers use – two teachers can behave in very similar ways but get very different outcomes because of the expectations that have built up around their teaching and around teaching in general.

There are limitless foci for research once we become sensitised to breaking down what we see. For example, we might become interested in gender in the classroom and what proportion of male/female students ask and answer questions. We might look at whether children with special needs are integrated into the classroom and whether teachers understand how to support individual students. We might look more philosophically at the authority of the teacher – very often teachers seem to exert their authority through the text book rather than seeking to explain concepts by first principles as the teacher does in our scenario. In doing all this we might become struck by not just how much teachers are required to do but how they have to keep a focus on so many things at the same time (e.g. Doyle, 1977). It is no wonder that teachers try to find routine in their work and that one lesson may look very like the next. Finally, we might in observing classrooms be intrigued by how much talk goes on and how central talk seems to be to teaching and learning. This we look at in more detail in the next section.

CLASSROOM TALK: TEACHER QUESTIONING

Classroom talk is a major focus for education researchers and we have already seen how teachers use talk for explaining, controlling and supporting students. Here we want to look at one specific aspect of teacher talk, questioning, in order to further illustrate the work of education researchers and how that work can translate into useful classroom guidance.

If you followed a teacher around for a day you cannot help but note that they ask a great many questions. Indeed, there is probably no other context in life where so many questions are asked. One estimate is that teachers ask questions for one-third of their class-room time with a total of, on average, 30,000 questions per year. So this is a fertile area of research. There are a great many ways of examining how questions are asked and what appears to be the purpose of asking them. For example, in classrooms, like the one in our scenario, we can see that questions were used in several ways: to gain and keep student attention ('Jools, what did I just say?'); to get students to articulate what they know ('What do we call it when we have very strong winds?' 'Does wind consist of any-thing?'); to stimulate curiosity and interest ('What intense wind movement have you seen?' 'When did you see this?'); to encourage thinking ('Can anyone tell me about the wind speed if the isobars on a weather map were quite far apart?'). Questions need to be broken down otherwise it is very difficult to understand how teach-ers can widen their repertoire in the classroom. Indeed, in seeking to understand questioning some researchers have asked whether questions are really questions at all. Often the teacher is not really expecting a detailed or thoughtful answer, they are using questions to signal that here is the direction in which the lesson is heading (Cotton, 1988). Here interaction between teacher and students may fall into a pattern of exchange known as IRF/E. The teacher *initi-ates* an interaction with a question ('can anyone tell me why the balloon has taken off?'), a student *responds* ('Yes it is the air coming out) and the teacher *evaluates* or gives *feedback* ('Yes that is right the air is coming out but what is happening is a rebalancing. a movement of air from high to low pressure spaces').

Researchers are interested too in the form that questions take (e.g. *Can anyone tell me?* versus *how/why do* questions) and who gets asked questions and who responds. In tackling the latter, researchers may be interested in whether boys get asked and answer more questions than girls in mixed classes (e.g. Duffy et al., 2001 looked at gender bias in student-teacher interactions) or how it feels to be a quiet student in a class. Researchers draw attention to open and closed questions too. For example, 'How does it feel to be in a gale?' is open while 'Is air pressure related to temperature?' is closed and requires a yes/no response.

Understanding language in the classroom is complex, and for us so fascinating, because much of it is dealing with relationships, assumptions about behaviour and the consequences of those assumptions. Relationships are not easy to describe for they are created in the mind of the individual: What am I expected to do in this situation? What does the other person expect me to do? What does this person imagine that I expect them to do? and so on. As an example, how do we really know what is an open or closed question. A closed question might turn out to be an unexpected trigger for detailed discussion or a means of offering insight into students' prior understanding – a closed question might not turn out to be closed after all. In contrast students often interpret an open-ended question as a prompt for giving the 'right answer' and after having asked the question and collected the answer the teacher moves on with the lesson in accordance with their planned agenda (Lemke, 1990). This can be seen in the IRF/E pattern we saw earlier. The IRF/E approach to questioning is not in itself wrong; it can help provide structure and direction to a lesson, but it can discourage students from actively participating in the classroom.

Questions can also be grouped by the cognitive demands made on the students. For example, questions may be broken down into ones that require *recall of information* (What did we just say about air temperature?) or *recall of facts* (Which weather systems tend to be hotter than others?) while *analysis* and *evaluation* may involve having to weigh up evidence (Where there is a greater distance between isobars what are the likely weather patterns?). Again, much depends on how these different questions types are interpreted.

Categorising is important work for educational researchers as it enables us to abstract strategies across a series of lessons; instead of talking about questions in geography or mathematics we can talk in general terms about the types of questioning that teachers ask. Of course, the balance of questions, and of question types, might look different in different subjects, and with suitable background knowledge we can explain why this is the case, but we cannot do anything unless we know what to look at.

Can we use this kind of detailed work to say what kind of questions work best? There are many attempts to do so and from our last chapter it is not surprising to discover meta-analysis studies that try to answer this question (Redfield & Rousseau, 1981 is an early example). In addition, all those with something to say about questioning will provide looser narrative accounts of what the literature shows (e.g. Walsh & Sattes, 2016). However, we should be careful how far we generalise as when it comes to questions so much will depend on the context; good teaching needs to take account of circumstances (e.g. the aims of the lesson and student readiness to engage with the topic) and should involve a fair degree of improvisation. What we can agree on is that research on teacher questioning can be used to widen practitioners' repertoires of question types and their understanding of questioning. In fact, in our experience, it is particularly challenging to develop questioning strategies. In working in teacher education, we were struck by how quickly many beginner teachers would take on the role of the teacher: they went from being diffident to assertive in the classroom; they found ways of putting concepts over to students, often in quite interactive ways; they could become consistent markers of students' course work. However, their questioning did not take off in the same way. It would have been impossible to provide useful guidance for these new teachers without using the research literature to show a range of available question types to help them plan and rehearse the questioning in advance of teaching. We also found it useful to discuss with new teachers the research on how long students are given to respond to questions – it is almost invariably too short. Probably the best-known idea emerging from this research is the concept of 'wait time'. Research by Rowe, first aired in 1970s, showed that most teachers wait only an average of 1.5 seconds after posing a question before either pressing for a response or offering it themselves (e.g. Rowe, 1974). Longer wait times can help to involve more students, and help develop deeper learning and avoid the 'guess what's in my head' approach. Using the research on questioning helped us develop quite practical advice such as: phrase questions clearly and at the right language level; make sure that questions are carefully sequenced; allow 'wait time' or pausing for responses; spread questions around the class or lecture room – look for a balance, such as back and front, male and female; draw ideas out from the learners and use praise for responses even if the answer to a closed question is incorrect; do not condemn answers to open questions purely because they do not coincide with 'what's in your head'.

The field of questions does not stand still and education research can inform new practice. For example over recent years there has been growing interest and research in the use of peer support when asking questions (e.g. turn to your partner and discuss your answer together, see Walsh & Sattes, 2016 earlier) and the use of clickers (and other low tech tools such as mini blackboards) to quickly collect and display whole class responses to questions (e.g. Tooth-haker, 2018, in the context of large undergraduate classes). Case studies on new practices will always be needed.

CLASSROOM TALK: CHILDREN TALKING

So far, we have looked at aspects of teacher talk in the classroom, and in particular the questioning they use. We want to keep on the subject of talk but now look at student talk. This is a very large field, which we cannot cover in any detail but we do want to look at the methods that at least some researchers use and we do this through a case study: *Talking and Thinking Together at Key Stage 1* (Littleton et al., 2005). This case study involved very young children (aged between 5–7) in schools in England.

The paper arose from the authors' concern to promote collaborative talk among students. This is a fascinating area as strong claims have been made for the cognitive and social value of collaborative talk but here the authors are arguing that it is the quality of the collaboration that counts, not collaboration in itself. If we are to discuss quality then, as we have seen with teacher questioning, we need a way of breaking down types of talk. The schema that the authors here have created is organised around three categories of talk: *disputational, cumulative* and *exploratory*.

Disputational talk is talk in which there is a lot of disagreement with everyone sticking to their original views. Little constructive criticism takes place. In cumulative talk learners do listen to each other but tend to accept and agree with what each other says. Here views are shared but they are not questioned. Exploratory talk is the big one. Here learners listen carefully to what other say; views are challenged but rather than going around in circles the group are trying to build on what has been said earlier and reach a shared understanding. The authors feel that exploratory talk is what education is about; for them it represents 'a distinctive social mode of thinking – a way of using language that is not only the embodiment of critical thinking, but also essential for successful participation in 'educated' communities of discourse'. However, they note that exploratory talk is underdeveloped in many classrooms and one explanation for this is that many teacher find it becomes more important to get through the lesson rather than give the time and space for deep reasoning to take place. A second explanation is that teachers might not know how to model such talk and how to support their students in learning how to listen or constructively disagree. Thus, their paper reports on the evaluation of projects that help teachers in modelling and supporting exploratory talk in classrooms. The project concerned six teachers (and their learning support assistants and headteachers) in three schools.

A key method in this work was analysis of video recordings of children's talk when they were asked to work together. The focus in this paper is on one group consisting of three children: Nuresha, Vijay and Kyle.

In the first recording, children are working together on a reasoning test. However, they found that Nuresha did not contribute to the discussion at all:

she can be seen sitting well back from the table, while the other group members, Vijay and Kyle, work on the task. Sometimes she looks round the room, sometimes she plays with her ruler but she is completely disengaged from the group. The teacher introduces the group task and asks questions to check for understanding. She asks Nuresha several questions, such as: 'Do you agree, Nuresha?' 'What do you think?' 'Can you see why it's not number 3?' In response, Nuresha nods. When the teacher leaves the group, Vijay takes over the pencil and answer sheet. Kyle says it is his 'go' and a little later asks Nuresha if she wants a go. Nuresha shakes her head.

(p. 176)

As for the talk between the two boys in the group, Kyle and Vijay, their interaction is described as 'disputational', not so much because they are arguing, but they are disengaged from the process of questioning each other and from trying to reaching some shared understanding.

The researchers go back to these children later in the project, after the teacher has discussed and modelled a new approach to collaborative working for the class. They are recorded again working on a reasoning task in which children have to decide which of six pieces fits into a pattern – this can best be explained as having to decide what piece goes into a jigsaw, but here the jigsaw is an abstract pattern and rather than manipulating physical pieces they are having to do this on paper. The video shows all members of the group leaning forward and frequently looking at each other as they work together. This time Nuresha is taking part throughout. The children discuss as a group how to handle the task and try to support their choices:

Extract 2:   *Which one . . .*
KYLE: Which one . . . (*to Nuresha*) You have to ask us which one we think.
    OK. You have to say: 'Kyle and Vijay, whose name, which one?'
VIJAY: You have to say 'I don't want to do this' or 'Kyle, what do you think? Say . . .
[*And a little later.*]

VIJAY: Next. Nuresha's getting the best ones, isn't she? You have to say 'what do you think, Vijay or Kyle?'

NURESHA: I think that [*number 2*].

KYLE: I think that [*number 4*].

VIJAY: Nuresha, look.

NURESHA: I think that ... that ... that.

KYLE: No, because, look, because that goes round. It goes out. It goes out.

VIJAY: Or that one.

KYLE: No, because it hasn't got squiggly lines.

VIJAY: It has to be that.

VIJAY: OK num' 4.

NURESHA: Num' 4.

The extract (Littleton et al., 2005: 178) shows all the children involved in the discussion as to which of the six pieces fits and agreeing it should be the fourth. They listen to each other and elicit other viewpoints. They explain the reasoning behind their choices ('that pattern goes round and round', 'that has not got squiggly lines'). They have not only reached the right solution but are able to explain why it is right.

In addition to these observations, researchers analysed specific words that some of the children used before and after the work that the teacher had carried out with the class on collaborative working. This showed that, after given guidance, children used the key words associated with exploratory discussion more – words such as covered *Because and 'cos* (used in explicit reasoning), *I think* (used to introduce hypothesis), *If* (used to reason about problems) plus *Why* and *What* questions too. The researchers also sought the reflections of teachers, language support assistants and headteachers from participating schools and this, they argue, revealed a strongly positive evaluation of the project.

What can we learn from this and similar case studies? Well, it emphasises the point made in the chapter that we cannot understand what is going on without categories to organise our observations; in this case, researchers needed to categorise children's talk in three ways and sought to exemplify all three types. Without these categories we can easily dismiss talk as unimportant or, in contrast, we can elevate its importance by believing that as long as students are talking, this is evidence that learning is taking place. Categorising talk enables a shift from talk in general to the quality of talk.

There are many other ways in which researchers categorise talk than the example presented here but whatever framework is used there is a balance between precision, or what researchers some-times call fidelity, or a fine-grained approach, and usefulness. In the paper discussed, the researchers have come up with a schema that is particularly straightforward to use in the classroom, and this is a strength, but it does oversimplify. There is also a more general problem too in any schema: how do we know what students really mean when they say something? Here the excerpts of chil-dren's talk do not stand alone, we are led to read them in par-ticular ways and that is fine if we trust that the researchers have been careful in interpreting what they see. But there is a wider question here as certain children are able to engage in exploratory talk at quite a sophisticated level as they have learnt the form it takes and the value that others place on it. Beneath the surface however they may only be superficially engaged with others and not prepared to change views at all; they are using talk strategi-cally. In contrast, less secure learners might want to stick to their guns (disputational talk) as to reconsider their opinions seems too threatening for the moment. But might they reconsider later? There is an assumption in much discourse analysis (this is a term to describe a general interest in analysing language) that all the significant learning takes place in the context of group interaction, but this is only part of the picture. There is more than one way of reading classroom talk.

In making recommendations for practice the authors make the obvious point that they would like to see more exploratory talk promoted in classrooms. They also suggest that we do not know enough about teacher strategies for promoting exploratory talk. This seems particularly important as no matter how productively students work together teachers need to know to push children's thinking along, for example how to support children to deal with errors (in the case study the children alighted on the corrected answer but what if they had not? Or what if they had been discuss-ing a problem for which there was no single correct answer?), or how to react when children reach their limits of understanding (for example, to go back to our first scenario, how to move children from intuitive notions of wind movement to scientific ones). They also make the less obvious point that we know much more about the value of talk than how to get institutions using exploratory talk. This brings us back to our first chapter on practitioner research: there are many well founded and properly research ideas about teaching that never make their way into practice.

EDUCATION LEADERSHIP: ANOTHER CONTEXT FOR CATEGORISING

We want to explore methodology further by moving beyond the teacher and students in the classroom and consider another field which has generated many different ways of categorising behaviour: this is education leadership. In fact, leadership studies became a major field of education research. This was a consequence of the growing realisation that leaders made a huge impact on student learning (Leithwood et al., 2008) but also reflected a growing desire by policy makers to have more control over education.

Case studies have provided a vocabulary for talking about the work of leadership. In some accounts there is an important distinction between leaders and leadership so that in the former the focus is on the people in leadership roles (principals, vice principals and heads of department) and in the latter a focus on leadership irrespective of who has the formal role. For example, in many institutions more experienced teachers may informally guide and support a new colleague and, for that matter, some designated leaders might do very little leading. There is also a very important distinction between leadership and management; leadership is much more about the vision for an institution, and the personal and professional values that the leaders are demonstrating, while management is much more about the day-to-day running of the school, i.e. ensuring that teacher absences are covered, students are entered for appropriate exams, reports are written, meetings are attended. One value of these studies is then to clarify what we mean when we talk of leadership and not surprisingly there is a great deal of debate as to how management and leadership should be balanced.

Case studies of leadership have come up with various typologies or classification of leadership and the different spheres in which leadership is enacted. For example there is a sphere of leadership that is focused on teaching and learning (*instructional* or *pedagogic leadership*); a style of leadership focused on radical change (*transformative leadership*); a *moral* leadership focusing on the values and ethics of leaders themselves; *participative leadership,* which seeks to involve all staff in the decision-making processes (this is aligned to ideas around *distributed leadership,* which reinforces the idea that leading is not the preserve of those in leadership roles). Recently there has been renewed interest in the idea of a *servant leadership,* which is sensitive to the needs of those being led and focuses on followers' development. Important in this research, and to be honest sometimes underplayed, is the importance of understanding the context in which leaders work. Leaders should be asking not only what kind of leader do I want to be, but what kind of leadership does this organisation need at this particular time? What kind of leadership best fits with these 'followers'? So there is a further category of *contextual leadership.*

The importance of this work on leadership is that it gives a way of understanding the various paths that are open to leaders and what might be the consequences of following these paths. Some attempts have been made to generalise about leadership based on literature reviews, and some researchers have drawn on PISA data too, but case study research offers an opportunity to provide detailed contextual pictures of leadership from which readers can draw their own conclusions. Indeed, if there is one sensible generalisation to make about leadership is that it is wrong to generalise. Rather, what seems to matter is the way decisions are taken more than the decisions themselves, and the confidence that both leaders and followers feel in the direction the institution is taking. We can have very successful schools offering different kinds of leadership if staff are comfortable with the way their work is organised, they feel listened to and their development supported.

We have touched already on some of the challenges in carrying out small-scale studies and want to explore these in the context of leadership study. In fact, compared to our account of classroom life, leadership is a particularly challenging area for research. Classrooms are complicated enough but at least the action is contained within four walls, within relatively short time slots. Leadership may happen over a much longer period of time and it might not be clear whose leadership should be looked at. There is, too, more and more focus on informal leadership rather than formal events such as staff meetings and annual reviews and by its very nature informal interaction is unpredictable.

We saw earlier that one methodological problem about education is that what people say about their actions might be different from how others see those actions. This raises questions of position and reliability. Consider, for example, the leader who describes him or herself as offering a participative and open style of leadership. This could be a reliable account of how their leadership is 'enacted' but then again it might not be. For example, the leader may prefer to represent their leadership as open and democratic as this is what is expected in their organisation and they do not want to admit publically that such a leadership style has been impossible for them to implement. Often, however, the leader may genuinely believe that they are participative and open and would be shaken to discover that others had a different view. Thus, it becomes important to triangulate (broadly compare and contrast) a leader's account of leadership with those who are being led. Here again difficulties arise. Researchers often asked followers about leaders but in practice many of these followers may have very little outright interaction with leaders or little to compare with. Feedback may be dominated by those with direct and untypical experiences. Thus, while it is important to triangulate perspectives on leadership, it is unlikely that all followers will offer the same view consistently. Some of these methodological challenges are raised in the following case study of leadership.

EXPLORING CULTURAL CONTEXT AND SCHOOL LEADERSHIP: A MODEL OF *CÓ UY* SCHOOL LEADERSHIP IN VIETNAM

Truong and Hallinger (2017) is a case study of leadership in schools in Vietnam. The authors note that leadership studies have largely evolved out of western English speaking contexts and worry that key categories have been transferred uncritically into very different systems. Thus, this study looked at Vietnam, which offers a distinctive political and school system. Vietnam is, first, a one party state in which leaders at all key levels of the state, including education, are party officials, and, second, it is an example of a country with a more collectivist culture and a greater acceptance of hierarchy, something often seen as typical in Confucian influenced cultures in East Asia.

This is a multi-site case study design looking at patterns of leadership within three institutions catering for different age groups: a teacher training colleague, a high school catering for 16–18-year-olds and secondary school for 12–15-year-olds. The schools, and the leadership in the schools was the focus for the study rather than the individual school principals. The schools were selected on grounds of convenience (i.e. researchers could gain access to the principals) but it is also suggested that they were typical of schools in Vietnam, though this is not explored in any detail.

The authors explain that two types of 'data triangulation' were employed. The first was 'perceptual triangulation', in which data collected from different informants (i.e. principals, vice-principals and teachers) were compared. When differences in perception were noted the authors used follow-up interviews to explore the cause of these differences in more detail. The second type of triangulation was 'method triangulation', in which data collected from interview, observation, document analysis and survey were compared both for consistency and divergence This enhanced the credibility of the findings.

Interviews were coded under four main nodes or themes: *exercising power, building relationships, decision-making* and *conflict managing and solving*. However, once the coding got underway, sub themes were created, which resulted in an extension and tidying up of the coding schema. This is a mix of top down coding, in that the researchers had key themes in mind, and bottom up coding to reflect what emerged during data analysis.

The paper then shows how leadership was enacted across the three sites. The key finding here is, first, the idea of Autocratic leadership. Teachers and principals both emphasised that principals had power over others and all stated the importance of attaining obedience, compliance and control. Again, both teachers and principals carried a high expectation of obedience and teachers accepted, without question, that 'the principal must be ready to use their position power to implement and enforce policies in support of the school mission'. The leaders themselves saw order, harmony and obedience to higher authorities as enabling the smooth running of the school. So far so clear. However, the authors also saw a second complementary but quite different line of discourse about leadership and this concerned the importance of moral character and prestige when leading others. Prestige referred to the 'moral quality, professional knowledge and inter-personal competence of the leader'. Leaders who were seen as prestigious faced less resistance and received greater effort, compliance, loyalty and respect from staff. Indeed, participants viewed moral quality as the most important personal characteristic of a leader. For example, the moral quality of leaders was more important than their competence as managers.

Thus, in this case study, leadership in the Vietnamese schools is not only autocratic it has to be earned by moral example and inter-personal skills – the authors describe this, borrowing a Vietnamese word, as *có uy* leadership, one that combines 'the use of legitimate and moral authority in order to achieve subordinates' obedience, trust, respect, commitment and emulation'.

The value of this paper is that it is gives an account of leadership that does not assume that western notions of leadership are applicable; context is very important in discussing leadership, not just the context of the school comes over, but the wider social, economic and political context that influences leadership. It also shows the importance of not just hearing what people have to say but dealing systematically with what they say, organising different accounts and checking for inconsistency and difficulties. A criticism of the study is that it is not clear how typical these case study sites are of schools in Vietnam, but this is for others to explore. There is, and this is not unusual in leadership studies, a tendency to talk about the effectiveness of leadership (here *có uy* leadership) without fully defining how we can assess that effectiveness. *Có uy* seems to be a very good fit to the expectations of the staff and principals but is that necessarily a good thing?

DOING A CASE STUDY

It is pretty clear by now that if we are to find a vocabulary for describing and explaining what is happening in education then we need to engage quite deeply with the contexts that we research. Unless we get close to what we are studying we will get a superficial picture and we will not understand the significance of what we see or the things that people tell us about. In fact, many of the contributions surrounding classroom talk and teacher explanation began life as case studies and in this section we want to discuss the contribution of case study to education research.

What is a case study? The term is generally used to refer to an in-depth exploration of a particular, often described as a bounded, context using largely qualitative methods (Stake, 1995). In a case study the researcher is not trying to present the general picture but to grasp the particular case. This helps to explain the 'how and why' of what is happening. Although case studies often use interviews and observation in order to get participants' perspectives on events (a so-called interpretivist aim), there is not a case study method, rather research methods can be tailored as to what is appropriate. Some studies, for example, draw on everyday conversations if they are able to access the context repeatedly and informally. Indeed observation (including shadowing of key informants) may be particularly important in looking at education as it enables researchers to compare the picture of classroom behaviour they have been given to the events they have observed. For example, when talking about wait times teachers often imagine they give students more time to answer than observation shows, and for that matter in many educational systems teachers describe themselves as talking for less than they do and being more learner-centred than observers would describe them as. (Of course, in some systems this may not be the case.) For a researcher this is not a question of catching the teacher out but a trigger for inquiry into the way that teachers see their role and the contextual pressures that may lead them to behave in a way that is different from how they had expected or wanted to. A lot can be deduced in the behaviour of the teachers and students but if our deductions are going to be credible, we need to get some input from teachers and some understanding of their positions, and a great deal of time and effort in education research goes into getting participant feedback.

In conducting case studies, it is important to explain why a particular setting has been chosen. Many are convenience studies (they are the ones that the researcher or research team can access as the case with children's talk earlier). They might, in addition, be selected as special, unique or outlier cases (for example, a case of teaching that has been praised by inspections, a case of a school with excellent use of technology) or, conversely, they may have been chosen because they are typical, sometimes called a key case of certain behaviour. Classifying the case in advance is never straightforward as you may not know what kind of case you are going to get. For example, the school that you were told was outstanding for maths teaching may turn out to be very ordinary – the reports may have been overoptimistic or key staff may have left and teaching 'reverted to the mean', i.e. ended up looking more like the 'average' school. On the other hand, the typical case may turn out not so typical after all.

Case studies can be single cases, taking place in one site, or multiple cases across sites. Here the opportunities and difficulties are balanced – multi sites allow you to get a broader picture, gaining awareness of consistency and inconsistencies across sites, but as time and resources are always limited if you go after too many sites you will end up getting a superficial view, thus defeating the value of case study in the first place. Perhaps it is better to focus on one and let others take on the work of comparison? Case studies are particularly useful for the work of classifying and categorising and, as seen earlier, the foundational work on teacher questioning and teacher knowledge were based on case study. Rather than the search for causality many case studies tend to show the consequences of action (for example what happens when certain questioning practices are taken up) rather than what causes these practices in the first place.

A NOTE ON THE WISDOM OF PRACTICE

Before leaving the classroom, we want to add a final note about teaching. Earlier we presented a productive example of a classroom:

the teacher commanded attention, she could explain some difficult ideas; she could get the students working together. We later saw a case study in which a teacher has successfully modelled and supported children's collaborative working. Styles of teaching were different but both tell us something about what teacher knowledge looks like and how it can be supported. There are in fact many ways in which educational researchers have tried to explain what teachers know and one of the founding figures here was Shulman (e.g. 1986).

On the basis of extensive classroom observation and interviews with teachers, Shulman identified different types of knowledge: *content knowledge* (what the teacher knows about, say, laws of physics; how to divide 200 by 4; why air moves); *general pedagogic knowledge* (for example, how to implement strategies such as collaborative working, how to form question types); *curriculum knowledge* (what is covered in various schemes of work); *knowledge of students themselves* (for example the strengths and gaps in knowledge that these particular students have); *the educational contexts* (for example the way the school works and the local community); the *ends and purpose of education* (for example what is useful for living in today's society).

Shulman's ideas have been debated and discussed in the intervening years and have found a new life in talking about the use of technology in teaching through the idea of technological, pedagogic, curriculum knowledge or TPCK (Mishra & Koehler, 2007). Like all good ideas about education, Shulman's schema is easy to describe and difficult to dispute: teaching is not only what you know about the subject, but about how you can combine different types of knowledge when, say, presenting a lesson or structuring a group activity. It is not enough for teachers to know, as in the example that began this chapter, the formal science behind weather patterns, they must also be adept at finding ways of putting the science over in ways to which the particular students in front of them can relate. Shulman's is a picture of teacher knowledge that practitioners easily recognise but would find difficult to articulate without the conceptual tools to do so. If we understand that good teachers have this rounded knowledge of teaching then this has a great many implications for those organising teacher training and the kind of activities that would really help teacher development. Thus, again we see that education research has very practical implications not just for the teachers themselves but for policy makers. In fact, policy makers often assume, and in many cases we believe wrongly, that content knowledge is more important than any other kind of knowledge and we come back to the idea that there are good ideas in education research that are not taken up.

SUMMARY

This chapter has taken us through the part that categorising plays in educational research and the idea that if we are to understand what is happening in, say, a classroom we need to classify the different actions, strategies and talk that we see. To do this requires sensitivity to what is important in teaching and learning, and, not least, a curiosity about teachers and teaching.

Providing categories to describe what we see may seem at times to make a very modest contribution to developing teaching and learning. But it is not. Without naming we cannot compare and contrast cases and we cannot make inferences about the consequences of doing things in particular ways. In this chapter we have focused on case studies in four areas of practice: teacher questioning; student talk; leadership and teacher knowledge. We have done this to provide an accessible context to describe case study methodology and to say something about more 'qualitative' approaches in general. There are of course plenty of other contexts we could have chosen.

In this chapter we see how challenging it is to carry out detailed classroom research. There is so much that goes into the classroom to which we are not party and much we will find difficult to understand. Thus, classroom and other case study often employ a mix of methods (so-called mixed methods research) and strategies of triangulation to reach more trustworthy accounts of practice.

FURTHER READING

If you are interested in the methodology of education research then we have already referenced some books at the end of Chapter 1.

There are, in addition, some clear guides to case study. For example, Gary Thomas's (2016) *How to Do Your Case Study* suggests that key questions in case study are: what kind of case it is; what purpose you have for carrying it out; what time period you are following; whether it is a single or multiple case study; what methods you will use and how you are going to analyse your data. This book is not specific to education research but is quite applicable to it.

We have referenced the idea of data coding earlier. A key distinction we have drawn attention to in this chapter is that between *bottom up* and *top down* approaches. On the former, Strauss and Corbin's (1990) *Basics of Qualitative Research* has been a key book. In fact, our example of watching a lesson that began this chapter was triggered by reading their account of observing what goes on in a restaurant (1990: 64). Strauss and Corbin want researchers to observe with an open mind but they are, in our view rightly, criticised for not drawing a distinction between openness as something to strive for and openness as a theoretical impossibility. Nonetheless, this particular book offers an exceptionally clear account of coding, including the generation of themes and categories in qualitative research. This is a general book and not confined to education or particularly about education.

If interested in the idea of leadership Bush and Glover's (2003) *School Leadership: Concepts and evidence* is dated but is very accessible and easily found online. You can find updates of their work in journals (e.g. Bush & Glover, 2014). Leadership is a very crowded field and there are many models offered by a great many other authors. There is also a lot to read about classroom management. Bill Rogers's (2011) *You Know the Fair Rule* remains a popular introduction, particularly in the context of teacher training, to positive, learning-centred approaches to managing a class.

The paper we cite on classroom collaboration belongs to a long tradition of educational research into children's talk. You can read more about this tradition in Mercer's (1995) *The Guided Construction of Knowledge: Talk amongst teachers and learners* and his more general book on language *Words and Minds: How we use language to think together* (Mercer, 2002).

Those looking at the 'cognitive' demands made on the students often call up Bloom's taxonomy – this was elaborated by Bloom and his collaborators and covered six major categories: *Knowledge, Comprehension, Application, Analysis, Synthesis* and *Evaluation*. This taxonomy has proved a productive starting point for many researchers and practitioners, not only for thinking about questioning but about curriculum design and assessment in general. Hanna (2007) is one out of many examples here. Bloom's taxonomy has been reproduced countless times and is openly accessible on thousands of online sites. A criticism of Bloom, or at least of those interpreting Bloom, has been a tendency to treating categories as discrete rather than joined up. For example, to be analytical you do need a good grounding in the knowledge associated with a subject.

5

EXPLAINING AND THEORISING IN EDUCATION RESEARCH

INTRODUCTION

One of the goals of education research is to explain teaching and learning and this chapter draws on the previous two chapters to show the different types of explanations researchers give. We look at the strengths and limitations of different research approaches and we argue that no single approach will give a full picture. The chapter then moves on to look at theory and theorising. Theory is a difficult, and perhaps off-putting, term but theory is needed to organise our thoughts about what we see. We explain types of theorising and their value. Finally, we look at the move towards a more interdisciplinary approach to education research and what other fields of research can do for education. This leads us to revisit the distinction between *research on* education and *research for* education. The chapter is organised around sections on explaining; theorising and explanation; illustrating theory; discussion of theory in education research; and interdisciplinarity.

EXPLAINING

When it comes to education research the search for explanation takes different forms. In Chapter 2 we saw that practitioners carry with them ideas about how their actions affect what is happening in the classroom, or other context for learning. These ideas are important in how teachers organise themselves and their teaching and are often described as personal knowledge (e.g. Eraut, 2010) as they are shaped by personal values, and individual experiences of teaching (or other work), in particular in the carrying out of day-to-day activities. Often personal knowledge is not fully articulated; indeed it may constitute a kind of folklore (*If I talk for too long the students will stop listening; Undergraduates will not come to 9.00 am lectures; Children are difficult to teach if they have just come straight from play time*), but folklore can carry important truths. Personal knowledge is both necessary and helpful but it can also be quite wide of the mark and we saw, again in Chapter 2, that there is value in looking at the problems of practice in more systematic ways. Being systematic means drawing on wider literature in planning and designing interventions and being organised in evaluating what has gone on. This kind of practitioner research can result in powerful explanations that marry personal knowledge and research evidence. But while there is plenty that can be generalised about teaching and learning from these accounts this is often not done.

In our next chapter we look at research that offers generalisations about teaching and learning. This kind of research enables propositions about education to be put forward that are applicable across contexts (e.g. *Investment in teacher development will result in improvements in learning; Visible teaching provides better learning; Formative feedback is central to effective teaching*). Sometimes these propositions are expressed loosely, for example *practitioners might like to consider* X *or* Y as sensible solutions to problems, but they are at times put more precisely, even mathematically (*strategy A will produce a larger effect size than strategy B*). The strength of this research is that it presents the big picture by aggregating many small case studies. However, a weakness is that those carrying out, and reading, this research can lose the detail and might end up believing in something about education without knowing the how or why, and without awareness of limitations and qualifications. This leads to a tendency for generalised research to be over-interpreted, for example policy makers, media and school leaders may see a certainty in the findings that researchers did not intend.

Large-scale general studies leave a gap, which smaller, more exploratory studies, often in partnership with practitioners, can address. In these studies, there is a focus on categorising what is observed or discussed. Here explanation cannot be divorced from the very important work of, what researchers often call, fine-grained description. Only by breaking down observations and actions into categories is it possible to compare and contrast the consequences of actions, for example, following different questioning strategies. The strength of these small-scale studies lies in the detail they offer and the opportunity to notice things that may not have been thought about before; a weakness or a criticism is that they are too local and are difficult to turn into specific guidance for practitioners.

These different approaches to education research offer different kinds of explanations and carry different strengths and limitations (see Table 5.1). This makes the argument that there is just one approach to education research, or one approach that should be elevated over another, just plain wrong. It also means that explanations researchers put forward never offer the whole picture, they are just one part of the picture.

THEORISING AND EXPLAINING

So far in this chapter we have talked about approaches to *explaining* education rather than *theorising* about education and we want now to go on to talk about education theory. We should begin by recognising that theorising can be off-putting as a term. Indeed, an old story is told of a minister in the French government, let us make him or her a Minister of Education, though similar stories can be told about officials in other fields and in other countries. One day a civil servant proudly brings him a solution to a problem, an apparently intractable problem that has dogged French education for a great many years. The minister looks at the plan unenthusiastically,

Table 5.1 Strengths and limitations in explanations offered within three different approaches

Approach	Typical methodologies	Typical explanations	This enables	But shortcomings are
Practitioner research	Action research, classroom study	There are strategies which can address particular problems of local practice	Practical orientation: problems of practice to be addressed	Tendency not to go beyond local context
			Encouragement for professional development	Overly descriptive
Generalising	Meta-analysis, systematic review, secondary data analysis	Certain variables (e.g. SES, visible teaching, formative feedback) affect outcomes	Identification of broad patterns which can give general insight	A tendency to 'over interpret'
			Identification of effective approaches/general difficulties	'How and why' is not clear
				May miss what is new or unexpected
Categorising	Case studies	Typologies of strategies (e.g. types of questioning; types of talk) and the consequences for using these strategies	A fine-grained description of what is happening	Small scale nature of the work
			A narrative around how learning (or other outcomes) is happening	Can become overly focused on descriptive rather than explanatory goals

coughs loudly and mutters, 'Yes, that is all very well, and looks like it might be an answer, but I am sorry can you run through with me how all this works in theory?'. The story is sometimes told in England in order to shine a light on the advantages of a practical approach to social research, and an Anglo-Saxon concern for dealing with problems, unencumbered by too much philosophical speculation. This is contrasted with a French intellectual tradition, in which theorising, at least in the view of its critics, gets in the way of dealing with difficulties and is carried out for its own sake. Perhaps the story has special relevance to education research for, as with other fields of professional practice, surely the goal of education research is to address practical problems (Evans, 2002), so why do we need to theorise? But we think that the Minister in the story had a point: if a solution is to work, we need to know why it will work, it has to have a theoretical basis. The question is not whether theory is in itself a good idea but what kind of theories should we put forward and what do they enable us to do? To go back to our earlier example, the personal knowledge practitioners bring to their work can be called *informal theory*; models of cause and effect relationship can be called *propositional theory*; ideas about how the system can be organised differently can be described as *critical theory*. Theory carries varying meanings (Krause, 2016).

Some social researchers have something else in mind when they talk about theories other than the examples we have given so far; they are thinking about more abstract ways of conceptualising what is going on. Theories become leaps of the imagination that go beyond categorising types of data or noting associations between variables (Hammond, 2018). Some theories are more speculative; they step back from the detail in order to establish a broad framework for understanding whatever is being researched. To illustrate the point, there are different explanations about how Socio-economic status (SES) is related to educational achievement and there are ways of thinking about the connection more *theoretically*, at least in more abstract and complex ways. One theory we could draw on is that of Bourdieu. And with Bourdieu we are back in the world of French speculative philosophy.

Bourdieu was a sociologist, rather than an educationalist, but he had an interest in education and, for that matter, quite sharp personal experiences of education, which affected him (Grenfell, 2004). He began his professional life looking at specific problems of ethnicity and class in Algeria before moving into more general sociology. Educationalists best know him for his broad interest in capital – by capital he meant 'accumulated labour' – and he wanted to encourage researchers to move beyond a single idea of capital (in popular shorthand, how much wealth you have) to an understanding of different types of capital: economic (tangible resource); social (contacts and networks); and cultural (education, qualifications and symbols of cultural distinction) (Bourdieu, 1986). He was interested in much more besides and his work, including his studies of capital, explored how far fields of social activity could be explained by looking at individual disposition and how far by social structure. Unsurprisingly, he was interested in the relationship of one to the other.

Bourdieu's interest in capital was seen, by some educational researchers at least, as a way of understanding class and learning outcomes (e.g. Reay, 2001). In particular it is the mix of these three types of capital that seems to lead many working class students to lose out: they do not have access to the physical resources that would give them more educational opportunity; they may lack the contacts to smooth their transition into higher education and work; they may lack the cultural references points that form a back drop to the curriculum. Bourdieu's theory introduces a level of complexity. It is more difficult to describe class in terms of three different types of capital than, say, occupation of a student's parents or, in some countries, proxy measures such as access to free school meals. And it is not easy to say how or why going to a theatre, rather than watching television, caries a sense of cultural discernment. However, with this more complete picture, researchers can put forward a rounded explanation of underachievement, and can better account for the association between SES and learning outcomes reported earlier. Even if useful theories are complicated, they are not difficult to grasp as they articulate what, at some level, we knew but had not really thought about.

It is then important to stress that theories do not represent a settled truth about, in our case, education, they invite us look at things in certain ways. This invitation seems only to get taken up when there is a time and place that makes the theory particularly relevant. In Chapter 2, for example, we saw that there were behaviourist theories based on simplistic ideas of mental conditioning. Perhaps these theories of learning felt timely when mass production was being introduced on a large scale. Workers were becoming increasingly deskilled and a key organisational problem was precisely how to condition them to carry out basic, repetitive tasks. In contrast, more constructivist approaches, described in Chapter 3, found a larger and more receptive audience when there were, post-second world war, increasingly large strata of professional workers who were expected to exercise their own judgement in dealing with complex problems. Constructivist theory better captured the creative aspect of learning and provided a better match for the spirit of the times.

Theories attract readers because of the power of the researcher's imagination, rarely because of the extent or even rigour of data analysis. In fact, very often theories are generated through reflection on very small-scale research, as with Thorndike earlier. Piaget, too, whose work on assimilation and adaption was ground breaking in the context of learning theory, drew in good part on studies of his own and a few colleagues' children in Geneva, Switzerland. Vygotsky, whose ideas as to how language is a tool for inner speech has been critically important in learning theory, built his theories around small-scale experiments in Russia. This is not to make a criticism. Theories start out small; they find life in their take-up by others or they slowly disappear, perhaps to reappear later when they have more relevance. Education is no different here to other areas of research.

Reflecting their more abstract nature, theories are often ambiguous. But as long as they are seen as containing something valuable, this ambiguity seems to encourage reflection and debate, rather than put other researchers off. For example, both Dewey and Vygotsky are not very difficult writers, but they are of their time and they can be read in different ways. Indeed, both have been read as offering a theory of learning based, on one hand, on direct, albeit communicatively sensitive, instruction to, on the other hand, an 'anything goes' student-centred progressivism. Theories should be taken as invitations to think and we should avoid theory wars of the type: 'my interpretation is better than yours'.

ILLUSTRATING THEORY

We conclude this section by looking critically at three examples that illustrate how theories can help us to think about education – we are not putting these particular theories on a pedestal, we could with more space have presented many more. The examples concern: deep and surface learning; situated learning and ecological development. We look at what they bring to how we look at problems and note their limitations.

LEARNING STYLES: DEEP AND SURFACE LEARNING

The first example is an odd one to choose as learning styles research has had a rather mixed press in recent years (e.g. Coffield et al., 2004). Learning styles researchers are usually interested in understanding difference at the individual level – rather than at the level of the social group, which is more the concern of sociology. In understanding individual difference, researchers have developed inventories (banks of questions) that operationalise (these questions taken together capture) key aspects of personality. For example, the Myers Briggs inventory is often seen as a reliable and useful measure to categorise people in terms of where they sit in respect to four scales: introversion to extroversion, thinking to feeling, sensing to intuition, and perceiving to judging. This enables the identification of 16 personality types and can be used as a diagnostic tool for individuals, a predictive tool for researchers and a practical tool for putting together mixed teams of collaborators. The transfer of personality styles to learning styles is problematic but various inventories have been used. Indeed, Coffield et al. (2004) found more than 70 different models of learning styles including: left versus right brain thinkers, holistic versus serialists, verbalisers versus visualisers and the widely used VARK categories (a preference for Visual, Audio, Reading or Kinaesthetic modes of learning).

The value of learning style research for education, almost irrespective of which inventory is used and how reliable it is, is that it can help sensitise the practitioner to the fact that there is not one type of student but several. With such awareness the practitioner can be encouraged to think about alternative ways to present information and set up classroom tasks. In fact, many argue that teaching is often geared to, and works best for, those who are able to follow spoken instructions and are comfortable with largely text-based assessment. However, this may not suit those with a preference for learning by practice or for doing rather than listening. This has led some to seek reform of education and for others to see greater value in informal education.

However, learning styles research has downsides. Categorising learning styles has little, what social scientists would call, ecological validity. That is to say you may be able, if asked to think about it abstractly, to identify your learning style preferences but once you get into particular contexts these preferences may change. You might, for example, be someone who is logical and procedural in the context of learning mathematics but intuitive in the context of learning drama. Or you may be extrovert in discussing topics in which you feel knowledgeable but introverted when faced with a topic you do not understand. A second problem is that even if teachers could reliably measure learning styles what are they supposed to do with this information? It could be argued that the goal of education is not to cater for a style of learning in which the student is strong but to increase their exposure to styles in which they are less comfortable, rather as footballers might learn to kick with their 'other foot' in order to move their game to another level.

However, there is one idea in learning styles theory, which we have found to be repeatedly useful. That is work by Entwistle, Malmo and Säljö, amongst others, on student orientation to learning (e.g. Entwistle et al., 1997). This goes back a long way. For example, Marton and Säljö (1976a, 1976b) asked university students to read an academic article, and to answer questions on what they had read. The students, it turned out, adopted either an approach that focused on *understanding* the content (as Malmo and Säljö put it, the 'structure of meaning') or one focused on *reproducing* the content, i.e. based on memorising unconnected pieces of information. The first was a deep learning approach based on what was 'signified by the text', the second, a surface-level processing approach based on the text itself, the 'sign' of the text (1974a: 7–8). Students following a deep approach understood more, could better answer questions and were later able to recall more about the text, than those following a surface learning approach.

Many studies have built upon Marton and Säljö's initial findings, and subsequent research has demonstrated that these different approaches to learning can be seen across a wide range of academic tasks. So, we have here the phenomenon of researchers producing a theory, in this case a theory about orientation to learning, generated in a small-scale study, and this theory becoming widely adopted and adapted. The important contribution in this learning styles work is that it helps practitioners in designing the curriculum. A deep or surface learning style is not a fixed attribute belonging to a student and identified by an inventory, but rather a response to how the task appears to the student in a real life setting. The implication, well observed over the years, is that surface learning happens because students expect assessment to be very largely carried out at a surface level, students are not themselves inherently shallow. So the critical question is an educational one: what can be done to encourage deep *learning* in our courses, rather than how do we cater for different *learners*. Here there are no easy solutions. For example, deep learning may imply creativity rather than memorisation, but memorisation is a feature of both the surface and the deep approaches. Deep learning requires creative responses but learners need to be able to use factual recall to spot gaps in arguments or compare the merits of two different arguments; in contrast in surface learning factual recall becomes an end in itself. This leaves many theoretical and practical questions open but deep and surface learning styles research shows us that an idea that began in psychology, and developed by educational psychologists, can be used to shine a light on teaching and learning and help us address critical questions in designing teaching.

BRONFENBRENNER AND AN ECOLOGICAL VIEW OF DEVELOPMENT

Our second example is a more mainstream one, at least in the field of child development: Bronfenbrenner's (1979) theory of ecological development.

The term ecological signals an interest in the ways in which development is shaped by context and Bronfenbrenner saw, at first from personal experience, that those studying child development needed to consider how the environment supported or limited the child. This concern led him to argue for naturalistic approaches to social research. He criticised mainstream psychology research for its artificiality, for example staging research into mother–child interactions in observation rooms rather than observing everyday contexts. However, naturalistic research did not tell the whole story of these interactions, the researcher needed to look at to what lay outside the immediate or micro setting.

Bronfenbrenner argued that child development takes place across different levels: *micro; meso; exo; macro;* and *chrono systems*. The micro level refers to direct experiences, for example, the interaction between a teacher/parent and a child. However, what happens at the micro level is shaped and influenced by other levels that may not be directly experienced: meso, exo, and macro systems. A meso system refers to the connections between micro systems (for example the way that a nursery school may report to, and involve, parents in its work). An exosystem covers ways in which a micro setting may be influenced by a wider organisational setting, for example how a teacher is influenced by a large school system. A macro system covers cultural assumptions that feed into each level of a system, for example, how cultural assumptions about childhood shape the way parents and teachers behave. Bronfenbrenner also introduced the idea of a chronosystem to focus on change over time.

Like all theories, Bronfenbrenner's framework has been adapted. For example, researchers at times collapse ideas of the exo into the meso system, and integrate discussion of the chronosystem into other levels, typically they do this for reasons of clarity. Of more concern is that some researchers have a tendency to see the child as a passive recipient of these various micro, meso and macro influences. In contrast, Bronfenbrenner's idea, elaborated more forcefully in later work was to see the child as in a state of active development and tasked with adapting imaginatively to the world. The world represented an objective reality but what mattered was how this reality was perceived as much as what it was (Bronfenbrenner, 1979: 4). The aim of child development in this sense was for the child to have growing agency, but this agency needed to be based on what was realistic in terms of the development and the child's understanding of what was possible.

Bronfenbrenner's ecological theory has extended beyond the particular field of child development as it gives researchers a more holistic way of understanding what is happening in a family, school or other world of activity. For example, if trying to intervene to change behaviour, ecological theory points to the need to address more than the micro level. Thus, initiatives to promote healthy lifestyles cannot simply seek to convince people of the merits of healthier food or more exercise; fresh food needs to be more easily available; there must better transport provision so that people are not reliant on cars; recreation areas need to be improved; classes and other interventions need to be accessible and so on (Cochrane & Davey, 2008). To seek change only at a micro level leaves innovators in individual classrooms exposed and ultimately having to give up on their innovations. In contrast change only at the policy level will result in policies that will only grudgingly be taken up in school or ones that are neglected altogether (see Fullan, 2007). Important too in ecological thinking is the importance of a wider cultural backdrop. For example, research into technology in education has generated many studies that show the value of particular approaches using specific tools. However, the widespread adoption of computers needs to be understood at a broader level that takes account of a cultural context in which technology is widely used at home, in work and for leisure and is heavily promoted by commercial providers. Explanations for the nature of ICT take-up also has to include recognition of periodic bouts of unrestrained optimism and moral panic concerning computers within the media.

The importance of an ecological approach is that education research often focuses on the small-scale (what is happening in the classroom, family or institution) or, alternatively, what is happening on a large-scale (in policy making or in the way that education is being debated). An ecological approach wants to do both: to look at how the system affects the individual and how the individual affects the system. It is a very difficult trick to pull off but Bronfenbrenner's theory gave use a starting point.

COMMUNITY OF PRACTICE

Community of practice (CoP) is an idea generated by Jean Lave, a social anthropologist, and Etienne Wenger, a 'social learning' theorist, and others, which has been extraordinarily influential in education research. The general idea in CoP is that learning is not *supported* by participation in communities; participation *is* learning; through participation community members are able to develop themselves. Over time, each community establishes ways of acting and behaving that become 'reified' (settled, and to some extent taken for granted), which helps the community to grow and develop. An important idea, at least in early attempts to define CoP, is that new participants learn participation via a process of 'legitimate peripheral participation', in which they first observe others, then carry out the more routine tasks, and finally reach full participation.

A CoP could be anything: a book group; a football team; a set of work colleagues; a class or a seminar group. Sometimes these groups evolve naturally out of shared interests, sometimes members are thrown together. This means that while CoP has been much adopted to look at learning in formal learning contexts, including online ones, it is much used too in the study of informal learning, including professional learning and apprenticeship. Indeed, Wenger's landmark book *Communities of Practice* is based, in part, on the everyday observation of 'Ariel', who works as a loss adjustor in an insurance company in America. He shows us how Ariel makes sense of her work, and addresses problems of practice, by negotiating and learning from others, rather than from formal training. For CoP researchers, learning always takes place in a particular context with other people (it is 'situated'); learning is not the work of a disembodied brain.

An early account by Jean Lave illustrates the nature of situated learning clearly (Lave, 1977). It concerned her participant-observation of tribal tailors in Liberia; research methods used included background interviews with tailors and their apprentices. Unusually in this field of research Lave conducted formal experiments and set the tailors a set of 32 hypothetical tailoring problems requiring basic knowledge of arithmetic for their solutions. These problems consisted of two types of questions: one type covered arithmetical problems typical of those that apprentices might encounter in their daily work ('tailoring problems'), and the other were more general ('non-tailoring problems'). Lave felt that most education researchers would assume that tailors lacking formal schooling would not be able to answer the non-tailoring problems as apprenticeship had too narrow a focus, i.e. you picked up a lot of mathematical skills while learning to tailor but these skills were restricted to the context of being a tailor. In fact, those with more extended schooling did do better on non-tailoring questions, but tailors without school experience were able to answer many of the more general questions and, for that matter, did equally well as those with schooling on tailoring questions. The findings made Lave wonder whether the more general education that school offers is as effective as often thought. She noted that apprenticeship training, which largely rested on observation and practice, was very different to the verbal instruction and context-free presentations of materials in schools. In other words, schools emphasised more abstract deductive teaching while informal learning contexts offered a more practical and inductive approach to learning. Apprenticeship may provide many more opportunities than previously assumed for transferable learning. This interest in situated learning was taken up in other studies not just of tailors but communities of midwives, quartermasters, butchers, and recovering alcoholics (e.g. Lave & Wenger, 1991).

CoP shares with other theories the idea of taking a fairly abstract principle and inviting us to look at learning in a new way. It also shares with other theories a capacity to generate much debate and controversy over the years. CoP has the great merit of seeing learning as situated and, in the process, explaining the value of informal learning. However, two criticisms, at least in some of the early work, are particularly powerful. First, CoP theory moves seamlessly from an 'is' to an 'ought': learning *does* take place in a community but does that mean it *ought to* take place in a community? From the educational research point of view what matters is not community but what kind of community and how can we describe, and support, communities in which valuable learning goes on rather than ones in which we learn little or simply have our prejudices confirmed. Here Fuller and Unwin (2004) make a distinction between expansive and restricted community in the field of professional learning and one feature of expansive learning is that members go outside their community settings to get new insight into their practice. There does not need to be a barrier between informal and formal learning, rather a recognition that both done well can produce good learning. Second, CoP seems to focus so much on members' social identity that their internal life is written out of the story. In fact, members of a community will act differently, feel differently and draw different conclusions from a CoP and indeed the same individuals will act and feel differently in the various communities in which they participate. Learning is social but it is also individual.

DISCUSSION OF THEORY IN EDUCATION RESEARCH

We wrap up this discussion of explanation and theorising by drawing out some conclusions regarding the way that theory works in education research. This takes in the role of agency and structure and the distinction between descriptive and prescriptive goals.

All education research, and social research more generally, works by drawing attention to what is important in an observation or event. Indeed, even very descriptive accounts of classroom life are heavily edited (or 'reduced') from a mass of material. Theorising takes this process of abstraction a step further and does so in order to transfer across contexts. Theories score highly when it comes to parsimony (the distilling of observations to key ideas) but less well in respect to fidelity (a comprehensive account of all that has been observed). Some theories try to offer greater fidelity (this often happens with modelling of data) but this can hinder the transferability to other contexts; theorists are always having to balance what is clear with what is comprehensive.

Theories enter and shape general discourse in powerful ways. For example, policy makers, practitioners, researchers and, at times, the general public use terms such as *deep learning, cultural capital* and *community of practice* to talk about educational issues. Powerful theories at heart are not difficult to understand and often readers of research reach the conclusion 'really, didn't we know that already?'. But the point is that we may have 'known' it already but it had not been articulated so clearly, or with such subtlety, before. Often theories seem to state the obvious because we are looking back; at the time it was not obvious and those proposing the theory may have felt, and been, quite isolated.

A further reflection on theories in social research is that they often contain a stance on agency and structure. For social researchers, agency looks broadly at the capacity of individuals to act independently and to make their own decisions. Structure refers to the ways in which society is organised (the distribution of wealth but also the functioning of social institutions and the nature of cultural expectations) and the effect this organisation has on the individual. Social research is concerned with both agency and structure but carries an inevitable tension as we cannot look at both at the same time (Eraut, 2010). The challenge for educational researchers, in particular, is that we are intensely interested in agency, not just agency in the sense of being able to do what one likes, but intelligent agency based on an awareness of one's situation, the range of available responses and the likely consequence of whatever decisions one makes. Intelligent agency is, in good part, the point of education, but it does mean that discourse about education can be unrealistically romantic. Here we are often swayed by books and films that tell stories about charismatic teachers and students. For example, *Lean on Me* was a popular 1989 US film that told the story of an outstanding teacher, played by Morgan Freeman, who by hard work and example had his students triumph over gang violence and budget cuts. *Billy Elliot* was a 2000 UK film concerning a boy who became a professional dancer in the face of family and community prejudice about his choice of career. More recently the Nobel prize winner Malala Yousafzai has been rightly feted for offering an inspiring example of overcoming extreme difficulty and achieving access to education. Education researchers are particularly susceptible to these accounts of agency as, like practitioners, they believe in the power of education to change lives; there would be little point in teaching or researching teaching otherwise. However, the explanations that education researchers put forward have to show awareness of structural limits. The value of ecological, or more broadly social psychology, approaches such as Bronfenbrenner earlier is that they offer a reminder of these limits without losing sight of the goal of education – to develop personal agency. In the real world the system will re-establish itself: charismatic teachers will leave difficult schools, girls will continue to be frustrated in their attempts to access education, certain children will lack the family and wider social support they need. It is not a question of putting agency ahead of structure or vice versa but how we balance the two.

This leaves a final challenge for researchers: whether they want to use their theories of education to be prescriptive or descriptive. Instinctively descriptive, the researcher's job is surely to explain what is happening not argue for or against something. Well, not entirely. As we see in our next chapter some education research is prescriptive as it directly advocates change, but all research is to some degree or another concerned with what should be done, as much as what is done. For example, the research on differentiated learning outcomes is based on an assumption that it is not acceptable for outcomes to be distorted by class, gender or ethnicity. Otherwise, it could be difficult to see what all the fuss, and consequent research activity, was about. The way we identify research questions, the way we interpret the data we collect in the course of our inquiries, the way we apportion responsibility, the way our research is read is inevitably value laden.

INTERDISCIPLINARITY AND EDUCATION RESEARCH

We leave this chapter with a final word on the distinctive character of education research.

Many of the theories used in education begin their lives in other disciplines. In our earlier examples learning styles research had roots in psychology; CoP emerged from cultural anthropology and organisational learning; ecological thinking was developed in the field of child development; theories of capital were developed in sociology and social theory. Is there anything that makes education stand out as a field or discipline in its own right or is it always on the receiving end of someone else's theory?

Few would disagree that conversation between different fields is important and helpful. As an example, a colleague once expressed, to a fellow academic in a Politics department, his disappointment that research findings were routinely ignored by policy makers, especially if the findings undermined government claims. This was particularly disappointing as the same policy makers would routinely claim that they were enacting 'evidence-based policy'. The academic in the Politics department was not impressed and simply said, 'Well, what did you expect?' and gave a much more sophisticated and realistic account of not only policy making, but the role of texts as policy documents than anything in the education literature. The example shows the value of taking ideas from other fields. Other researchers will fill in our gaps in knowledge as they have approached a question from a different direction.

In fact, over the course of our careers we (the authors) have noticed a closer relationship between education and other disciplines and a greater willingness by education researchers to go outside their areas of comfort. This is valuable but the relationship between disciplines can feel quite clunky at times. For example, there are many case studies of teaching and learning coming from education researchers that are quite descriptive accounts of practice until they suddenly change track with references to Bourdieu, or whoever else is fashionable, as a way of establishing a 'theoretical underpinning'. We have not only read this kind of paper many times but produced some of our own. Something more is needed if research is going to draw on the insights developed in other disciplines. Concepts cannot be taken off the peg, they need to be reworked and reapplied. This process of adaption was illustrated in our three examples concerning deep learning, CoP and ecological frameworks. We finish with two further examples to show just how difficult it is sometimes for education researchers to access research in other disciplines, even when that work concerns teaching and learning.

The first concerns Education Neuroscience. This research brings together scientists and educationalists to explain 'how the brain works', at least in respect to how neurons and neural circuits function. It has taken off as a field of study in good part because the technology now exists to provide pictures of brain activity (the most sophisticated examples concern functional Magnetic Resonance Imaging or fMRI, known to the lay person as 'brain scans', though less intrusive are geodesic electrode nets that sit on the head of the 'subject'). It is an open question as to how intrusive or accessible scanning is as a research tool, but facilities can be hired and research carried out in ways that were unimaginable in the past. Supplied with pictures of brain activity (though we should think of these not as pictures but maps) we can assess development and learning. In particular the argument goes:

a   Given we know what part of the brain does what (for example we know that frontal lobe areas are associated with 'executive functions' such as exercising planning and self control; the right hand side of the brain is associated with logic and left side more with tasks to do with creativity and the arts), and

b   Given we can map development in areas of the brain, including changes in activity in these areas in response to certain triggers or activities, then

c   We should be able to get an idea of how an individual is developing, and the nature of any disabling conditions. More controversially we should also be able to show the impact of certain interventions through pre- and post-scanning of brain activity.

Scanning has many applications in medical science where its use can be life changing and there are applications of neuroscience in education which seem to be productive and helpful. For example, neuroimaging research can show that some children diagnosed with dyslexia have reduced activation in regions of the brain known to be associated with awareness of word structure (Howard Jones, 2014). This helps to show that there is biological basis for the condition of dyslexia and with such knowledge teachers and parents could get a better understanding of the difficulties certain children face and go on to design more appropriate support. In similar ways imaging can show reduced development in certain regions of the brain when looking at conditions such as autism. Imaging has also shown the physical changes of the brain as we get older and the biological basis for declining mental abilities. Research is clearly at an early stage and there is much that we do not understand but in principle there is value in exploring connections between neuroscience and education.

However, the value of such collaboration is limited when education neuroscience is not addressing educational problems. For example, there are quite a few studies in neuroscience which look at how sleep is related to brain activity. In one such study (Molfese et al., 2013) researchers looked at whether children's performance in simple tests to do with attention, speech perception and executive function dropped when children went to bed an hour later and experienced 'minor sleep restriction'. These changes were measured using geodesic nets. This kind of research has a disciplinary logic but it offers little of interest to education and we can guess the weary response from an audience of education practitioners when presented with the 'news' that better patterns of sleep may make their students more receptive to learning at school. In fact, the measuring of change is not our problem; rather, the critical question for parents, teachers and students is to understand why some young people miss out on adequate sleep and what can be done about it. For good measure we cannot think of any education researchers who would find the experiment, albeit one on minor sleep deprivation, ethically acceptable.

Our second example returns to the theme of inequality and education outcome. Here the different foci of education and sociology become clear in a study, *Learning to Labour* (Willis, 1977), carried out some years ago in the UK, but periodically revisited internationally for its sociological insight. The book is an ethnographic study (a study which drew on close participant observation) of 12 working class boys or 'lads' from a school in Birmingham, UK, conducted over 2 years in the early 1970s. It wanted to look not only at the lads' perspectives on schooling but to chase their journey into factory jobs. Willis found that the lads were not interested in school seeing it as 'middle class' and education as not 'masculine'. He found many examples of counter cultural behaviour: messing about, getting into trouble with teachers, acts of petty vandalism. One reason for these perspectives on school was that the lads envisaged getting manual work for which formal qualifications were not needed. In fact, a strength of the study was its longitudinal time frame so that Willis followed them for a further six months after they had left school. Predictably, work turned out to be less satisfying and secure than the lads had expected. Willis writes of a resistance to school which turned out to be self-defeating, for they ended up with restricted opportunities as young adults.

Learning to Labour is a fascinating book on the sociology of education and sheds light on aspects of the educational experience that have been taken up by sociologists many times since. It offers an interesting theoretical take on the issues of agency and structure, which we looked at earlier. However, it is a book driven by questions of sociology not questions of education. Practitioners are rarely interested in reading that there are students who do not attend school or that there are students who can be rude to teachers and resistant to learning, because, to use a sociological phrase, it is their 'lived experience'. Practitioners want to know what they can do about it. And there is little in the book to help. Working across disciplines is fine, but rather than borrowing from these disciplines wholesale, education researchers need to consider findings from an educational viewpoint. This is not about putting one field of study ahead of another but recognising different fields of study ask different questions for different reasons. What is distinctive about education research, and why it is not the sociology of education or the psychology of education, is that education research always brings us back to change and how we can support intelligent change; it is research *for* education not *about* education.

FURTHER READING

This chapter has covered a lot of ground and the list of further reading is long, so be selective.

If interested in the ways in which social theory influences education discourses you could try Mark Murphy's (2013) edited *Social Theory and Education Research* – this does have a specific focus on four thinkers, including Bourdieu, though does draw out some general issues. Michael Grenfell's (2004) *Pierre Bourdieu: Agent provocateur* gives a readable introduction to Bourdieu.

Allen Repko and Rick Szostak's (2017) *Interdisciplinary Research: Process and theory* is a very practical guide to carrying out research across disciplines. It is a general book for social researchers, rather than one aimed at education. (In looking at research across different fields some key terms are: *Crossdisciplinary*, involving a team from different disciplines working together but hanging on to their own discipline standpoints; *Interdisciplinary*, involving a deeper level of exchange between disciplines leading to a shift of boundaries in one's own disciplines; *Transdisciplinary*, a full-on willingness to engage with problems rather than disciplines and to create new conceptions of knowledge.)

Even though it is not the latest contribution to the field, Stephen Billett's (edited) (2010) *Learning Through Practice: Models, traditions, orientations and approaches* gives a good overview of debates in professional learning.

Bronfenbrenner's (1979) seminal book is the *Ecology of Human Development*. It is very readable and thought provoking. Another broadly ecological account widely taken up in education is Activity Theory (e.g. Engeström et al., 2002).

As regards learning styles, this report by Coffield et al. (2004) *Should We Be Using Learning Styles? What research has to say to practice* gives a good critical background and is still relevant today.

There is so much written on CoP in education. You might want to go back to the original contribution by Jean Lave and Etienne Wenger: *Situated Learning: Legitimate peripheral participation* (1991) and Wenger's *Communities of Practice* (1998). Both Lave and Wenger write very clearly, perhaps, as remarked in reference to Strauss and Corbin at the end of Chapter 3, this is one reason for their extensive take up.

On deep learning, Ference Marton, Dai Hounsell and Noel Entwistle's (1997) *The Experience of Learning: Implications for teaching and studying in higher education*, kickstarted several debates – the book is free to access online at the Institute of Academic Development at the University of Edinburgh, at least at the time of writing.

Malala Yousafzai's (with Patricia McCormick) (2014) *I am Malala: How one girl stood up for education and changed the world* is a very readable and moving story.

6

ADVOCATING

SAYING HOW IT COULD BE OTHERWISE

INTRODUCTION

Most education researchers set out to describe what is happening in schools, places of work, within families and so on. The focus is on *how things are* (description) rather than starting from an idea, or developing an idea, as to *how things should be done* (prescription). Of course, a researcher's values and pre-conceived ideas about education will interfere with how they look at a problem and why they identify a problem as a problem in the first place. However, the researcher is trying to minimise these affects (sometimes researchers talk about 'bracketing' or putting to one side their values and beliefs) with the aim of achieving as an objective an account as possible. Of course, they, or at least the vast majority, would not claim to achieve objectivity but the point is that they are striving for it. In contrast some researchers want to show how things ought to be and compare present reality to that ideal, drawing attention to gaps and shortcomings in present arrangements. In this chapter we look at some of the most frequently aired perspectives on how education is going wrong and how education ought to change. The chapter is organised around six perspectives: neoliberal; conservative; liberal; reformist;

progressive; and radical and it is followed by a discussion of what can be learnt from advocacy.

NEOLIBERALISM AND EDUCATION

Neoliberalism builds on the concept of economic liberalism – the belief in free markets that was core to the global economic and technological revolutions of the nineteenth and twentieth centuries. Classical economic liberalism carried the idea that individuals were the best judge of their own interests and needs, and this meant that they were best served by markets which would respond to what they wanted. Markets were dynamic. Offers were tested in the market place: new products could be established; suppliers who gave the public what they wanted were rewarded; unsuccessful offers were withdrawn. In other words, if consumers wanted more apples and fewer pears, the market would provide more of the former, fewer of the latter. This was not only a more efficient mechanism for delivering what people wanted but the market was a morally superior mechanism as, rather than imposing goods and services on individuals, it responded to consumer demand.

So why *neo* (or new) *liberalism*? The challenge for liberal economists in the twentieth century was to adjust to a world in which many governments were managing their economies in much more interventionist ways, and providing social goods and services of their own. State intervention was undermining the working of the market mechanisms – a state of affairs that the public accepted and in many cases welcomed. Neoliberals such as Hayek (1944) wanted to tackle the public's sense of complacency and found their views increasingly influential. One reason for this growing influence was that economies turned out to be more difficult to manage than many governments had thought. Another significant factor was globalisation. In a world in which there was freer movement of capital and people, individual governments felt less able or willing to take responsibility for providing services. Neoliberalism was about reaffirming the benefits of the free market but also about seeking free markets into areas of social life operating under different rules. In addition, neoliberals tended to offer a less complicated version of needs and wants than classical liberalism, quite simply what the public wanted the public should get.

As regards education, the defining goal of neoliberals was to extend free markets across all sectors. This meant defending the existing private sector and promoting further private provision, or at least market like competition between schools, colleges and universities. Neoliberalism was based on the simple, and intuitively appealing idea, that popular institutions should be rewarded and unpopular ones penalised. As such it proved attractive for many governments, even ones not associated traditionally with conservative or right-of-centre policies, as competition seemed a means to revitalise public goods and services.

An obvious challenge in operating education as a market was how to ensure that education should be open to everyone. This led to attempts to influence the market by, for example, the use of education vouchers in several countries (a 'voucher' could be used by a parent or adult learner as a guarantee of government funding at whatever institution they chose) and the promotion of hybrid funding models, such as Charter schools, which did not charge fees but were, to some extent at least, independent of state control. In principle, vouchers and other schemes provided equality in the market, but in practice not all consumers were equal. Some parents and carers had less clout as their children had special needs, which were expensive to address, and systems of regulation were introduced to limit the freedom of schools to choose their students.

A further challenge in extending the market was to ask how the consumer (this posed a wider question of course, who was the consumer?) was going to judge the quality of provision? In a market place a consumer would make a calculation based on value for money, but if education were free, money did not come into it. A proxy 'unit of currency' was needed. Learning outcomes seemed the obvious answer and high stakes tests were introduced in many national systems while internationally PISA enabled global comparisons to be made. With such testing policy makers could create performance matrices. It was more complicated to compare higher education providers but global university league tables, ranking providers according to reputation, employment prospects and other measures, were constructed, often by global media companies.

The cause of neoliberalism has been largely taken up by the radical right, but suspicion of state control of education goes wider. Long ago Ivan Illich (1973) critiqued schools as institutions and argued, presciently, that there was another way: learners could be matched and share learning together in open networks. He later denied this had anything to do with neoliberalism but it tapped into a belief that education was in much better hands if the consumer was in control. Such ideal market conditions can exist online where there are growing markets for learning exchange, particularly for language teaching, and a wide range of open access MOOCs (Massive Online Open Courses). Freedom to choose has been taken up in a growing home schooling movement and for that matter across time progressives have frequently set up their own private schools in opposition to prevailing practice.

PRIVATE EDUCATION IS GOOD FOR THE POOR

The idea of extending the free market in education is often seen as privileging those with capital but Tooley and Dixon (2005) looked at private schools in the education of the poor in India, Ghana, Nigeria, and Kenya. They noted that the number of low cost private schools was growing and these schools were playing 'an important, if unsung, role in reaching the poor and satisfying their educational needs, in areas of urban deprivation and villages' (Tooley & Dixon, 2005: 1). The poor, or at least some of the poor, were taking their children out of government schools, which they saw as not meeting their children's needs, and moving them to unaided private schools that were. This was the market at work. And these private schools were, it was argued, out-performing state schools on many measures: they had more generous pupil-teacher ratios, higher teacher commitment, and sometimes better facilities than government schools and better outcomes. Teacher salaries were a key issue in the viability of such schools, teachers were paid considerably less than in government schools but seemed to be more committed and doing a better job. Many low cost private schools tried to be equitable in terms of gender intake and examples of schools subsidising the very poorest with concessional places were given.

The strongest argument in neoliberalism is the claim that in the absence of anything like a free market mechanism what is the incentive for institutions to improve performance: why should institutions tailor their offer to meet the needs of their customers, if they already have a captive market. Only the market can ensure higher levels of consumer satisfaction and better learning outcomes. It is at heart a pragmatic argument: the market works and, moreover, state provision works better when it introduces elements of competition.

Critics of neoliberalism focus on free market experiments with mixed or negative results and the decline of the school as serving the public good (e.g. Labaree, 2018). The state may have given up direct control of education but put in its place a complex system of checks, balances and regulation. By competing with each other, rather than cooperating, institutions, particularly in higher education, are spending ever-growing sums on marketing, which could be better spent on provision. Critics are sceptical about the validity of measuring learning outcomes and note that these do not take in the more holistic criteria by which parents, practitioners and children judge their schools. They see little appetite for further marketisation and neoliberalism as an imposition. Bottom up initiatives such as low cost education in India are quite a different thing from the take-over of public schools by large corporations. It has also been claimed that, at least as regards India, the very poorest cannot access low cost schools, disadvantaging and denying access to those from large families and/or low caste families (Härmä, 2009). Finally, critics argue that public education can be both responsive and efficient through democratic mechanisms and normal pattern of regulation.

CONSERVATISM AND EDUCATION

Politically those who are self-defined as Conservative are often aligned, or sympathetic, to the neoliberal position described earlier and stand on platforms that seek to extend the market in schools. However, the conservative tradition in education is something broader and more diverse. Indeed, if conservatism means being averse or resistant to change then conservatives might be instinctively resistant to the disruptive policies that neo-liberals promote.

Conservatism arises in different contexts. For example, in East Asian systems the Confucian legacy provides a backdrop to conservative thinking around education, in that it stresses harmony, cooperation and honour to parents and elders. Those writing from a western tradition have a rather different notion of conservatism, one that shares a concern for respecting the past, but is more focused on the curriculum. Here conservatives often argue for a core curriculum, held within strong subject boundaries, which all students should follow. Conservatives, too, stress the central role of direct instruction in the classroom rather than learning by doing or learning by induction – as an example, they often want to see more focused teaching of phonics to young children (this concerns identifying and manipulating 'phonemes', or units of sound) rather than whole language instruction (a focus on the whole word and the meaning of the word). Finally, many conservatives have a concern for rigorous testing. They argue it is patronising to suggest that those without basic knowledge and skills have the same life chances as others; they do not.

Conservative educationalists need not be politically conservative. For example, the German-born philosopher Hannah Arendt, whose work is difficult to categorise but held liberal values on many issues, wrote in praise of conservatism in education. For her the problem was that educational thinking, she was thinking of the USA where she lived most of her life, had been hijacked by progressives' ideas from continental Europe. She saw three problems (Arendt, 1961).

The first was that we had romanticised the child's view of the world and ended up believing that the 'society formed among children' should, as far as possible, be autonomous and children left to govern themselves. This, for her, was not only a misinterpretation of childhood but a positive danger as children could behave to each other in a way that was far worse than the 'the severest authority' of the teacher. There was no place for child-centred learning, there was a gap between teacher and child in terms of experience and knowledge and that was one reason we had teachers and schools. Teachers, of course, should help children find their own way in the world, but they should do this slowly and not pretend that the world is like the child wants it to be.

Second, as regards teaching, like other conservative thinkers, Arendt thought that a training in subject knowledge was important, but this was being downgraded in favour of a science of pedagogy. She wanted nothing to detract from knowledge as the source of teacher authority.

Third, there was, at least in respect to young children, an over-celebration of play as if play was the 'most appropriate way' for the child to behave in school. Education had got to involve the learning of abstract ideas, teachers needed to show children principles and concepts, which went beyond what they could glean for themselves through direct experience.

Arendt wanted to keep school a distinctive and special area of childhood experience. Schools were not there to reflect society, rather teachers were custodians of knowledge and ways of behaving that had been handed down over time. The same point is put eloquently by the English philosopher Michael Oakeshott, who, in a much cited passage, argued that education was a transaction between the generations, education:

> involves the transmission through the curriculum of the main features of a civilisation, so that people grow up knowing where they have come from and what the past achievements of their society and of humankind have been. Education is therefore a dialogue with the past. It is not a space within which unformed children are encouraged to recreate the world afresh. That may come later, if they choose, when they are adults and citizens, but can only take place on the basis of an understanding of what has been and what is.
>
> (Oakeshott, 1989: 93)

Oakeshott highlights here the profound concern in conservative writing for giving children access to an inherited world of meaning.

HIRSCH AND EDUCATION

One writer who has become a well cited as a conservative critic of 'progressive' education is E. D. Hirsch. He has written several books on education and the key arguments are refined and extended over time but his thinking was exemplified in his best seller *The Schools We Need* (1996).

He saw schools in the USA, Hirsch focused on the USA but his ideas have been taken up internationally, as going drastically wrong. He believed that educationalists were overly influenced by 'discredited' theories of education based on a romantic view of childhood and an anti-knowledge culture in schools.

What made Hirsch a powerful protagonist for the conservative position is that he tried, at least at times, to be pragmatic. For example, he called out the knee jerk responses that both conservatives and liberals make about education in the USA and argued that it was possible to take arguments on their merits; for example, he described himself as socially liberal but educationally conservative. He also claimed his conservative agenda was not concerned with selection and maintaining privilege but with underachievement among the socially disadvantaged, including disproportionate numbers of black children, and he wanted all children to succeed. He proposed a common curriculum, and was not impressed by free market neoliberal solutions. He argued that all children needed to gain the ability to read, write and communicate clearly, and unless they had a core knowledge of science and culture, they would not be able to participate, economically and culturally, in society.

Core knowledge was key for Hirsch and teaching this core knowledge was more important than so-called generic skills, or higher order skills, as all advanced skills rested upon prior knowledge. Without memory and recall children were not given a hook on which to hang new ideas. He was critical of the argument that technology had made memorisation and knowledge of facts redundant – see reformism later – there were things we did need to commit to memory so that they became automatic. He argued too for a core curriculum on pragmatic grounds as it meant that children had common experiences on which to build when they moved classes or, as often happened, when they moved school.

PROS AND CONS OF A CONSERVATIVE POSITION

The key strength in the conservative position is that it values schools as a special realm of childhood experience providing access to abstract ideas that set children up for life. Conservatives argue that teachers do children a disservice if they pander to their whims and interests and it is no good pretending children know more than they do. Schools do not need to reflect what is current and what is fashionable, teachers should exude self belief in their authority and the authority that their understanding of the past gives them. Conservatives see themselves as bringing realism and rigour into education debates.

What are the weaknesses in the conservative position? It is often criticised as a belief in drill and practice learning, authoritarianism in teaching and an uncritical acceptance of order. This is unfair, but if such caricature is to be avoided conservatives need to offer pragmatic guidance for teaching and learning. In particular they need a theory to show how instructional teaching can be both rigorous and engaging. It is simply odd to see subject knowledge and pedagogical knowledge as somehow opposed to each other as in Arendt – see Shulman's wisdom of practice earlier in the book. What is wrong about thinking how teaching can be developed in imaginative and engaging ways? Conservatives believe that schools know what is good for the child, teachers are not there to entertain. But surely good teaching is responsive to students? Conservatives need to say more on what they want such mastery of core concepts to lead to. They explicitly want children to become independent thinkers but that goal seems pushed forward into the future; how will students acquire independent habits of thought without continued rehearsal from a young age? Finally, as regards subject knowledge, conservative argue forcefully for being cautious or 'conservative' about curriculum reform, for example, introducing changes to reflect our multicultural society, but there is no value in a rigid adherence to a past curriculum for its own sake.

LIBERALISM AND EDUCATION

There are many different versions of liberalism and some liberal writers we discuss might as easily be used in support of conservatism or progressivism. However, liberalism is presented as a strand in its own right due to its special concern for the manner by which students learn, for self-interrogation and for equality.

Liberal education takes the moral dimension seriously. Education is not just about what we learn but the way we learn and the kind of people we become. Confucius (551–479 BC) was cited as conservative influence in education, but his concern for moral values also made him a liberal educationalist, long before we thought of liberalism as an idea. For Confucius, it was only through cultivating a concern for truth, honesty and respect that you could be a good student; learning and moral character went hand in hand (Sheng, 2018). Many years later we find the English liberal philosopher Mill (1806–73) addressing the same theme. He drew a distinction between 'lower' and 'higher' pleasures. For Mill, education lay at the heart of understanding how to live a good life; through education we can cultivate higher pleasures, for example a sense of the aesthetic or an understanding of moral virtue (Ryan, 2011). Life was not about satisfying base pleasures. Mill was economically liberal, but unlike purist neoliberals, he could not accept that what the people wanted they should have, it was rather that through education people will come to want what they do not yet know that they want.

In terms of teaching and learning, a liberal education tries to develop a capacity for reflection and self-interrogation. Ideas should not be accepted on the basis of tradition or superstition. This inquiring spirit dates back to Socrates (c. 470–399 BC), or at least the Socrates that Plato presents (Plato, 2005). Socrates taught through dialogue and sought to guide his students to follow the logic of their arguments. As a teacher Socrates was slow to put forward his own ideas and wanted to help his interlocutors to question their own beliefs. They often ended up wiser, albeit without a clear resolution to the questions they first asked. Of course, liberal teaching does not need to be in the form of Socratic dialogue, but reflection and the exercise of reason are hallmarks.

More radical versions move liberal education from reflection to reflexivity. In other words, we should not simply reflect on our ideas to step back and think about where these ideas came from in the first place (reflexivity). Mezirow (1997), for example, valued adult education for its transformative potential, making him something of a radical educationalist, but his concern for questioning what is taken for granted and to make our own interpretations rather than rely on others makes him typically liberal. He draws on the German philosopher Habermas to contrast instrumental learning aimed at advancing your self interest with communicative learning, which aimed to help you understand your purposes, values, beliefs, and feelings. For Mezirow, adult learning always came with learning to think as 'autonomous, responsible persons'.

A third distinctive feature of liberalism is its concern for equality. Of course, all the other positions we discuss in this chapter start out from an assumption that education should be open to all, but equality has its roots in the liberal values of the Enlightenment – the intellectual movement of the eighteenth and nineteenth centuries. According to Enlightenment thinkers we share a common humanity and we are equally deserving of access to education. In Mill, for example, this meant that anyone who neglected the education of their children violated the rights of the child – this applied both to girls and to boys. But our sense of shared humanity goes further; for the philosopher Kant we are all moral agents with a capacity to exercise reason and free will. This means that we respect the views of others, and we should treat others and extend to others what we ourselves enjoy.

JOHN DEWEY

Dewey (1859–1952) was a USA philosopher and educationalist. He was a reformer, and in some ways a progressive (though this was a label he rejected), but he was also a liberal as he did not want students to passively accept claims to knowledge, all such claims needed to be put to the test. How could students do this? By tackling problems. In wider society adults faced a broad range of naturally occurring problems in their everyday lives, but in school it was different. Teachers needed to intervene in school in order to present children with the same breadth of problems that adults faced. Dewey wanted a curriculum in which children experienced problems, tried to address these problems, and drew conclusions through reflection on their encounters with these problems. Problems were really important for Dewey, not so much for the problem itself, but as rehearsals for addressing the 'indeterminate' situations (ones that were unpredictable with no single solution) that they would meet in real life. For Dewey thinking:

> begins in what may fairly enough be called a forked-road situation, a situation which is ambiguous, which presents a dilemma, which proposes alternatives.... In the suspense of uncertainty, we metaphorically climb a tree; we try to find some standpoint from which we may survey additional facts and, getting a more commanding view of the situation, may decide how the facts stand related to one another.
>
> (1910: 11)

One way of 'metaphorically climbing the tree' might mean looking at the ideas and concepts that had been handed down from the past – Dewey was not dismissive of subject knowledge, and he did not believe that students needed to discover key ideas from scratch. Rather, Dewey believed that whatever ideas students came up with needed to be tested; whether these solutions 'worked' or not, only became clear by experimentation, i.e. when the consequences of following a course of action were considered. In assessing these consequences students could not rely on their own subjective opinion they needed to discuss with each other. Dewey wanted education to provide a rehearsal for the intelligent and collaborative action needed for all aspects of adult life, it was preparation for a way of thinking.

PROS AND CONS OF LIBERALISM

The value of spelling out liberalism as a distinct perspective on education is that it sets out a moral purpose for education, and a critique of narrow 'possessive individualism' (i.e. a calculation of economic self-interest) within some versions of neoliberalism. Education is developmental; children are not 'naturally good' but educational experiences can make them more curious, more rounded, more able to identify personally fulfilling ways of living their lives and to have the confidence and capacity to act on their choices. Liberal conservatives share some of this, but liberals want education to provide a rehearsal for the exercise of problem solving and critical thinking. This rehearsal should happen from the start of education, it cannot be put off. A liberal education cannot be judged on accredited learning outcomes or international testing, these may be important but they are not the whole picture. Liberalism tells us that *learning* as a verb covers more than gaining knowledge of something; it takes in how you gain that knowledge. For example, suppose there was a pill you could take that enabled you to speak another language, or you could learn the rudiments of geology under hypnosis. You may have required certain knowledge and skills in these ways but you have not *learnt* anything; learning requires effort, discrimination and the exercise of a conscious will.

Criticisms come from both conservatives and, as we see later, radicals. Conservatives see liberal education as weak when it comes to covering a core curriculum and accuses it of diluting the instructional role of the teacher. In terms of pedagogy, liberalism could be criticised as 'going around the houses' when at times what is needed is controlled practice. Radicals see in liberalism a weak form of social equality; liberals take seriously the idea of equal right to education but they do not challenge head-on the social inequality that skews the work of schools and other institutions.

REFORMISM AND EDUCATION

All efforts at advocacy are reformist in that it is seeking to change education. However, in this section we concentrate on a recurring reformist idea: how to make the curriculum more relevant to young people.

We begin with a book that attracted an unexpectedly large following, extending beyond the USA where it was written, in the early 1960s. *How Children Fail* provided observations about teaching and observing teachers and children by John Holt (1923–85). Holt (1964) felt that schools were failing and they were failing because of 'fear, boredom, and confusion'. Much of the curriculum was irrelevant, trivial, and dull and students did not understand the relevance of what they were learning. For Holt, a focus on subject teaching was sucking the life out of teaching; children's curiosity and sense of discovery was being suppressed. He concluded that teachers needed to stimulate children's imagination and creativity by making the curriculum more meaningful, more playful, and more relevant.

Holt offers many examples of dry instructional teaching. For example, he described a teacher leading the class through an exercise at the board, one that requires children to identify which words go into which grammatical column: was the word a verb, adjective or noun? He found the activity had little relevance for the children and they turned to strategies that allowed them to pretend to understand without engaging in learning at all. In the classroom he reported that:

> There was a good deal of the tried-and-true strategy of *guess-and-look*, in which you start to say a word, all the while scrutinising the teacher's face to see whether you are on the right track or not. With most teachers, no further strategies are needed. This one was more poker-faced than most, so *guess-and-look* wasn't working very well. Still, the percentage of hits was remarkably high, especially since it was clear to me from the way the children were talking and acting that they hadn't a notion of what nouns, adjectives and verbs were. Finally, one child said, 'Miss –, you shouldn't point to the answer each time'. The teacher was surprised, and asked what she meant. The child said, 'Well, you don't exactly *point*, but you kind of stand next to the answer'. This was no clearer, since the teacher had been standing still. But after a while, as the class went on, I thought I saw what the girl meant. Since the teacher wrote each word down in its proper column, she was, in a way, getting herself ready to write, pointing herself at the place where she would soon be writing. From the angle of her body to the blackboard the children picked up a subtle clue to the correct answer.
>
> (Holt, 1964: 15)

This lesson was teaching formal knowledge for its own sake and in the circumstances, children were reduced to game playing. This in a nutshell was contemporary education for you!

Holt was in many ways a progressive (see progressivism, later) but he set up a clear challenge that has been addressed by mainstream educational reformers ever since: how can we make the curriculum more relevant? For contemporary reformers, any solution to this question lies in understanding the ways in which our ideas about knowledge (what counts as knowledge and how knowledge is created) has changed and continues to change. For example, for the OECD in the new knowledge economies:

> memorization of facts and procedures is not enough for success. Educated workers need a conceptual understanding of complex concepts, and the ability to work with them creatively to generate new ideas, new theories, new products, and new knowledge. They need to be able critically to evaluate what they read, be able to express themselves clearly both verbally and in writing, and understand scientific and mathematical thinking. They need to learn integrated and usable knowledge, rather than the sets of compartmentalised and de-contextualised facts. They need to be able to take responsibility for their own continuing, life-long learning. Students must be able to use technology to learn content and skills – so that they know how to learn, think critically, solve problems, use information, communicate, innovate and collaborate.
>
> (Centre for Education Research and Innovation, 2008:1)

There is here a happy convergence of liberal ideas about education (with its concern for problem solving and dialogue) with hard-headed realism about what modern economies need. And there have been numerous attempts in many educational systems to make this marriage work – for example, by giving young people work experiences; offering vocational routes; encouraging interdisciplinary and promoting a more professionally oriented higher education. At various times interventions have stressed teamwork and collaborative learning and students have developed skills of reporting to particular communities and stakeholders (see Gardiner, 2017, earlier). However, reform has a long way to go and much of the curriculum in many countries feels out of date, boxed into traditional subject settings, with students taught through abstract and formal methods. Fullan and Langworthy, for example, echo Holt in making their case for curriculum change. They argue that:

> students are increasingly bored in school and ever more so as they go
> from grade to grade ... For teachers one could say that there's only one
> thing worse than being bored and that is 'having to teach the bored.'
> Because students are bored teachers are bored too and the system is
> 'pushing' students and teachers out of school.
>
> (2013: 23)

One very obvious way in which schools have not reformed lies in the use of technology (Dede, 2010). Most young people, in contexts in which they have access, spend a great deal of leisure time interacting with each other through social networks and accessing information and entertainment over the internet. Rather than working with this interest schools often seem to want to shut out technology, for example by offering pen and paper tests measuring abstract, routine skills. When teachers adopt technology, it is to tame it, for example, by using Interactive White Boards for instructional teaching, rather than for supporting a more collaborative, and perhaps more playful curriculum. There is something in technology that, as Cuban (2001) puts it, does not suit 'the grammar of schooling' leaving computers 'oversold and underused'.

For Fullan and Langworthy, Dede and many others what is needed is problem solving plus technology – problem solving as it creates a purpose for teaching and learning and technology as it not only motivates but it enables access to all sort of new ways of working that would not be possible otherwise. For example, with technology it is argued students can access large, sets of constantly updated data; communicate within and across schools, create interactive presentations for diverse audiences; set up applications of control in stimulated real life settings. According to Fullan the new curriculum needs to showcase new competences such as critical thinking, creativity, communication and collaboration.

PROS AND CONS OF REFORMISM

The strength of this reform agenda is very clear: it offers to address the mismatch between the curriculum and the kinds of knowledge, higher order skills and attitudes of independence and flexibility that are needed to participate in contemporary social life and in economic life. A refreshed curriculum would better meet the interests of young people and avoid the boredom of abstract formal learning. It is an agenda that is capable of gaining widespread acceptance, including support from reform minded employers and liberal progressives. Reforms in teaching and learning have often been well received though difficult to maintain.

The reform agenda is attacked by conservatives, including Hirsch, for diluting the teaching of a core curriculum but perhaps their stronger argument is that reformers have been misreading the nature of transferable skills. Conservatives see traditional academic knowledge as transferable because it is abstract. In contrast, what is learnt in more practical and applied ways might be more restricted in respect to context. This argument was explicitly addressed in Lave's case study of Liberian tailors when discussing CoP in Chapter 5. But a point not often picked up in discussing Lave is that abstract knowledge about mathematics was not redundant, it was transferable to tailoring contexts even if not learnt in those contexts. There is some support in PISA data too – see earlier – that those students, or rather those schools, which were successful in teaching traditional subject skills were also doing well in terms of collaborative problem solving; the former did not need to be at the expense of the latter.

Two further criticisms. From the Left, it is argued that if curriculum reform becomes too closely tied to the idea of meeting economic needs this could represent a very restricted kind of learning. In practice only in certain sectors do high skilled information processing jobs appear, much work is becoming more repetitive and deskilled, what implications does this have for a more vocational curriculum? Second, and a more general criticism, is that reform has been too closely associated with the use of technology; for critics it seems particularly difficult for teachers and schools to adopt technology and the gains of doing so have been difficult to document.

PROGRESSIVISM AND EDUCATION

Progressive is a disputed label but used here to signal a concern for a strongly child-centred approach in which play and direct physical experience in and outside the classroom are particularly valued.

The guiding principles of progressive education date back to the eighteenth- and nineteenth-century Europe, as they do for the liberal perspective on education. However rather than a celebration of modernity, progressivism was a backlash against industrialisation and a reaffirmation of what was 'natural' and innocent. In part, progressive educators shared with Romantic poets such as William Blake (1757–1827) and Whitman (1819–92) a sense of 'awe and wonder' about childhood and discomfort about how childhood was changing. In part, progressives were also a product of liberal Enlightenment thinking and the idea that we were all capable of exercising reason and had the right to work out our life goals for ourselves. Such a right needed to be extended to children. Children were not empty vessels but had a capacity for reasoning and that needed to be respected and cultivated (Reese, 2001).

In progressive thinking, teachers provided the experiences that enabled children to learn – teachers were not redundant but they did have to think carefully how and when to intervene. Progressives wanted children to have freedom to explore, and this often meant experience of the world outside the classroom, rather than of 'stuffy classrooms' in which children sat in rows. Progressives wanted to entrust education 'to the eternal powers of nature herself' and they spoke, in varying degrees, of how the child should grow up in harmony with their instincts. The aim was to educate the whole child – intellectual education was only part of a wider plan; Pestalozzi (1746–1827) for example, wanted to keep an equilibrium between three elements: hands, heart and head.

Progressives wanted to avoid inflicting unnatural influence on the child and this meant that the approach to teaching was inductive. Rather than being taught general principles children should work these principles out for themselves. Pestalozzi (1894) argued that children should learn through activity and many progressives provided their children with experiences of play, drawing, talk and manipulating objects. For Fröbel (1782–1852) play was a creative activity and through it, children become aware of their place in the world. Children should not be given ready-made answers but should arrive at answers themselves. Progressives did not have inventories of learning styles but they did see each child as unique and striking their own educational path.

MARIA MONTESSORI

Many of the ideas we come to know as progressive education today derive from Montessori (1870–1952), an Italian educator and activist. Montessori's initial studies were in medicine and as her interest in education grew, she started teaching children with disabilities. Her success with these children led her work on more general principles in education. She developed a teaching programme and, over the years, acquired an international following.

In Maria Montessori's writing many of the themes of progressive education were revisited and extended. The idea of education was again seen as cultivating a child's natural development. There was a concern too for a 'holistic' education. She was keen on children working with materials, in particular clay; she stressed the importance of good diet and of overall cleanliness and hygiene; she wanted children to experience the outdoors and bring the outdoors into the school by having school vegetable gardens. She wanted education to cover all of the senses, the young child should learn to discriminate by touch, smell, sound, taste and sight. Moral character was developed alongside intellectual understanding. She wrote of the importance of nature for in nature the child saw 'a mirror of themselves'.

Montessori believed that children should not sit in rows, they should be free to move and to talk, they should wear loose clothes not ones that restricted their movement. The furniture and materials in a classroom should be in proportion to the child. All education should take place at the pace of the child; the child would naturally develop if their curiosity was allowed to flourish. Once that curiosity was aroused there was no need for rewards and punishments, indeed children lost interest in them.

The teacher was there to observe the child, not to restrict them. This implied the teacher did not do anything at all but this is not the full story. For example, one reason that the teacher observed a child was to understand that child and know what kind of activities they would benefit from. Montessori called her approach one of scientific pedagogy and this required a practice of observation and experimentation. The teacher was not there to dominate but she might explain, in a 'calm and simple' manner, and lead the child into certain exercises. The child would grasp concepts when they were ready to and when they had seen and practised enough – for Montessori the art of the teacher lay in:

> knowing how to measure the action by which we help the young child's personality to develop. To one whose attitude is right, little children soon reveal profound individual differences which call for very different kinds of help from the teacher. Some of them require almost no intervention on her part, while others demand actual teaching. It is necessary, therefore, that the teaching shall be rigorously guided by the principle of limiting to the greatest possible point the active intervention of the educator.
>
> (Montessori, 1913: 231)

Montessori saw development as natural and was optimistic about the child's curiosity and capacity for self-development and self-control. However, the teacher had to maintain order. This she did through example and working with the child not against the child – this approach worked so well that good order came to be taken for granted. However, Montessori did not see the child as naturally good and recognised that individual children might do things that upset the rights of others. Then the teacher needed to step in.

INFLUENCE OF PROGRESSIVISM

Progressivism is mostly discussed in the context of early childhood and many of the things for which Montessori argued are mainstream in kindergartens and primary schools – not simply ones that bear the name Montessori. This influence can also be seen in contemporary Forest School initiatives aimed at promoting learning through woodland and other outdoor experiences. While progressivism was seen by many conservative writers as the great affliction of twentieth-century education, full blown progressivism in the sense of a romantic belief in the natural innocence of the child can only be seen in small-scale teaching experiments and a small number of experimental schools.

In looking for progressive principles in other sectors the name Carl Rogers (1902–87) is often cited. Like earlier progressive thinkers he saw education as a developmental process in which learners come to understand themselves and their values. However, his background was in 'client-centred therapy' in which the aim was to help clients develop the confidence to identify for themselves possible solutions to their problems. He saw some of these counselling techniques as very important in adult education (or andragogy as he called it) and wanted to the teacher to practise techniques such as 'active listening' (Rogers, 1969).

PROS AND CONS OF PROGRESSIVISM

The strength of progressivism is that it demands that parents, teachers and society as a whole take children and children's rights seriously. For example, the United Nations Convention on the Rights of the Child (Human Rights: Office of the High Commissioner, 1989) was not itself a progressive manifesto but it does take seriously the idea that the child has rights (for example a right to a life, to be free of discrimination, a right for development, and a right to have views respected), for which progressives carried out the intellectual ground work. Progressives might be presenting a myth of a naturally inquisitive and creative child but do we want teachers who see the point of teaching as that of grinding down the child until he or she accepts domination as routine? Progressives were the first to cite the importance of play in child development.

Having said that, progressive writing is sentimentalised. There is a belief in the natural unfolding of knowledge that critics see as unlikely and an imagined seamless transition from practical experience to abstract concept, which is suspect. The teacher can surely exercise authority without being authoritarian. This is not just a criticism coming from conservatives but was one reason why Dewey was not a progressive. There is also much dogma in nearly all progressive writers, for example, a rigid model as to how and when to intervene, which is off putting and out-of-kilter with the spirit of progressivism.

RADICALISM AND EDUCATION

Radicalism, like reformism, refers to many different strands of thought, but here we look at radicalism from the Left, or at least a radical liberalism. A defining feature of radicalism is its concern for the relationship of education systems to society; radicalism sees inequalities in power in society and education itself as heavily influenced by these inequalities and even contributing to them. Radicals want to challenge the way things are done.

Carrying out educational change is of course easier if you change society first. For example, Ghandi proposed an anticolonial education that would break free of the British or English curriculum, once India had been liberated, and Bukharin and Preobrazhensky (1920) imagined a completely new education system, one which extended education to all and had a more social and proletarian character, in post-revolutionary Russia. But what should radicals do before such momentous social change takes place, how should teaching and learning be conducted in unequal and oppressive societies? Here Freire (1921–97) is a key influence. Freire's core work concerned literacy and like many others he saw illiteracy as a barrier to understanding and participation in society. But learning to read and write was not enough, the poor needed to understand why their lives were so difficult. This link between education and fighting injustice was particularly clear to Freire as his ideas were first worked out in Brazil in raw and oppressive conditions: high levels of poverty and unemployment; high levels of illiteracy; periodic and oppressive military rule. Under such conditions, literacy could not be defined by the technical capacity to decode texts; rather, for those at the margins of society, it involved understanding what is was that oppressed them, and how to engage with others to challenge this oppression. For Freire, tackling literacy came with a commitment to develop 'conscientização' or conscientisation, a word used unevenly but (using the gendered language of the time):

> the process in which men, not as recipients, but as knowing subjects, achieve a deepening awareness both of the sociocultural reality that shapes their lives and of their capacity to transform that reality.
>
> (Freire, 1970: 221–222)

In the field of literacy conscientisation could be developed by critically reviewing the 'deceit and propaganda' in everyday images and written texts. This meant reviewing the materials used in literacy manuals and replacing them with ones that were more realistic and would stimulate critical discussion. Working together adult learners could learn literacy skills while setting out on a journey to change society for the better.

The idea of conscientisation has inspired social activism in many contexts, in particular across Latin America but also globally. For example, Cervantes-Soon (2017) reports on the dire social circumstances of young women in low-income areas of Ciudad Juarez, in Mexico. She wrote of high level of militarisation, with battles between the army and the drug cartels, very high levels of abuse in the home and of rape, and gender related murders. How can education respond? Her account was optimistic. She showed the steps one school was taking, and the work young women were doing, to develop a spirit of activism and resistance. Taking a stand was a twofold process. An external battle to demand the right to take part in civic activities but also an internal battle for the young women in her study to learn to respect themselves as they were by rejecting dominant discourses about gender.

DECOLONISING THE CURRICULUM

The idea of decolonising the curriculum has brought together different types of criticisms in an overall complaint about power imbalances inside education. First, decolonisers want to challenge institutional bias. For example, they critique structures that restrict the representation of women and ethnic minorities in leadership positions. They draw attention to economic interests, which make neoliberal universities too eager to put knowledge at the service of the highest bidder and too slow to 'speak truth to power'. They question cultural power in campaigns such as *Rhodes Must Fall* (this was directed against the continuing presence of statues to British colonisers on South African campuses but led to more general protests and indeed to an international movement, Chantiluke et al., 2018). Second, decolonisers want to critique the curriculum. For example, they want teachers and students to question ingrained ideas of what should be taught and to have greater awareness of the way that racial and gender stereotypes are transmitted. At times this means questioning the language of instruction too. Third, decolonisers want to develop a research methodology built around equitable relationship with the communities that are being researched.

DECOLONISING METHODOLOGY

This account (Keane, Khupe, & Seehawer, 2017) from science educators in South Africa provides examples of how indigenous knowledge could be respected in the school science curriculum and how a new curriculum could bring benefit to the local community. They briefly describe the participatory projects they carried out – for example, one involved the setting up of a chicken farm project, which helped students understand basic natural science while addressing community needs. They describe strategies for showing respect and giving back to the community. These strategies covered the participation and mentoring of local unemployed youth to serve as co-researchers; the involvement of NGOs to support projects and assist with training and access; and continual discussion with community elders, teachers and students, wherever possible in local languages. Researchers were also careful to feed back their findings and did so in appropriate ways. For example, in one case, a community-wide festival, co-hosted by the researchers and the local 'induna' (or chief) showcased research outcomes through 'songs, dance, story, drama, photos, drawings, speeches by elders'. Researchers were also careful to produce teaching materials and research reports written in local languages and to contribute to community newspapers.

PROS AND CONS OF RADICALISM

The strength of radicalism is that it draws attention to imbalances within education systems at every level and as with action research tries to do something to address them. Radicals ask: Whose knowledge is promoted?; Whose voices are heard?; Whose skills are valued. They unsettle the complacency within education systems. Radicals draw on liberalism to show that we share a common humanity, but they see this liberal idea of equality as hollow in a world in which there are inequalities that not only define how resources are distributed but dominate the way we think of ourselves and our idea of self-worth.

Radical positions provoke conservatives who see a slippery slope leading from open debate about the merits, or otherwise, of traditional texts into a curriculum based on partisan standpoints and identity politics. More subtly, liberals, and indeed those within radical pedagogy, worry about who is leading transformative learning. For example, in Freire there is an assumption that literacy should lead to the radical restructuring of society, but literacy gives you a capacity to make up your own mind about what oppression is and what is your place in the world. Freire does not always recognise this.

ADVOCACY: VALUE; METHODS AND DIFFICULTIES

The value of discussing advocacy is to show the big ideas that are held about education and the how different writers take very different positions on teachers, students and the conduct of teaching and learning (see Table 6.1). For the conservative, knowledge is abstract and academic; teachers have authority; teaching is deductive. But for progressives, knowledge is practical; teachers stand to the side; learning is inductive. For radicals, everything comes down to inequality in society, for reformers, it is about the curriculum and for neoliberals it is all about free markets. For liberals, education is about the cultivation of reason.

With a better understanding of these different positions we can see that the issues raised about teaching and learning in the previous chapters in a new light. To give three examples. Earlier, in Chapter 3, we found complaints about an excessive focus on high stakes testing. These complaints can now be seen through the lens of advocacy. For liberals, education should not, or not solely, be judged in terms of instrumental understanding; developing autonomy and self-understanding are also important and these cannot be so easily measured. While for reformers, the focus on conventional testing is simply embedding an outdated curriculum and for radicals the hidden purpose of testing is to differentiate children into categories of class. In Chapter 4 we later saw work carried out to describe teacher strategies such as questioning and controlling students. These strategies are core to a science of pedagogy but we can see them as all but useless from the perspective of conservatives such as Arendt, and misguided in principle by progressives who do not believe in instructional teaching. Finally, in Chapter 5 we saw a discussion of deep learning. Not much to worry about there from a liberal point of view, but surface learning is not really a bad strategy for *learning*; it should not even be described as learning.

Some will, of course, critique advocacy as it seems to involve offering subjective positions on what should be done about education without a firm basis in fact. For sure, advocacy research comes with weaknesses both in its use of data and the coherence of argument (see column 6 in Table 6.1). But advocacy research is not simply 'making it all up'. Advocates draw on a range of experiences. Writers such as Mill and Pestalozzi use their own rather distinctive experiences of early education to generalise about teaching and learning – something social scientists would call autoethnography. Writers such as Hurt, Froebel, Pestalozzi and Freire were practical teachers, Montessori an outstanding one. Dewey helped set up an experimental school and spoke regularly to practitioners and teacher unions and Hirsch engaged heavily with teachers in the Core Knowledge Foundation. Those advocating change often know at first hand what they are talking about. Further, in offering their own interpretations of education, advocacy researchers are doing what theorists have always done: taking a leap of the imagination (see Chapter 5). There is a fallacy in social research, as there is in natural research, that if the researchers have used objective measurements, then the interpretations of the data, not just the data, are reliable. But this is simply not so. Theories are always guesswork, a disciplined guesswork calling on data for support, but still guesswork. Advocacy calls up different kinds of data. These data provide evidence that is more personal, more impressionistic but the conclusions are to be taken seriously.

DIFFICULTIES WITH ADVOCACY

Having described its value, some advocacy, it has to be admitted, is undoubtedly difficult to engage with. Writers often start out along

Table 6.1 Summary of five positions on education in respect to teaching, teachers and students

These positions	Have as a big idea	See teachers (and schools and higher education) as	See students as	See teaching as	A key criticism
Neoliberalism	The market rewards good providers and bars bad providers	Responding to market demand	In higher education: rational, seeking to develop their economic potential Parents/carers as rational decision makers on behalf of their children	Measured objectively in test scores	Education not a conventional market
Conservativism	Core knowledge is handed down from the past, such knowledge is needed for independent thought and economic participation	Having authority by greater knowledge and experience	Governed by passions which need to be managed	Deductive: abstract principles need to be explained and practised Teaching organised around traditional subjects	Excuses dry didactic teaching of an outdated curriculum

continued

Table 6.1 Continued

These positions	Have as a big idea	See teachers (and schools and higher education) as	See students as	See teaching as	A key criticism
Liberalism	How you learn is as important as what you learn	Exercising authority through questioning and setting of appropriate activity	Influenced by past experiences, capable of moral and intellectual development	Inductive: ideas are drawn out by activity and questioning Teacher works alongside students Peer support helpful	Overcommitted to inductive methods
Reformism	The curriculum needs updating	Aiding the student to develop understanding and self-efficacy to live and work in contemporary world	Bored and disillusioned with a curriculum stuck in the past	Digitally rich, built around authentic or simulated real world problems and promoting core competences	Traditional subject knowledge is transferable

Progressivism	Work with the child not against the child	Observant, responsive to children's developmental needs	Meaning makers, curious, in a state of development	Inductive, in which play and physical experience are valued Peer support offered	Sentimental and over-romanticised view of the learner
Radicalism	The world is unjust, give the less powerful a voice	Leaders and facilitators	Oppressed, needing to understand the causes of oppression	Working with students to achieve change	Whose version of freedom is being offered?

the lines of 'we are going to hell in a handcart'. Holt sees *all children* as bored, not some children, some of the time, or boredom as a condition of childhood, but school is irretrievably boring. Arendt sees progressive education in America as overthrowing 'all traditions and all the established methods of teaching and learning' from 'one day to the next'. Quite an achievement! Hirsch believes that scholars from abroad are 'astonished' that children in the USA 'actually as competent as they manage to be'. Here writers are playing the game that if readers can accept how desperate things are, then they will be more open to whatever is being advocated as the solution. Hence schools are failing, *therefore* the answer must lie in neoliberalism; children are bored, *therefore* the answer must lie, ultimately, in home schooling; standards are falling, *therefore* the answer lies in a core curriculum; the curriculum is out of date, *therefore* we should use technology to update it. This is not helpful.

We need to find a way of discussing education with humility and acceptance that we might be wrong. There is room for compromise and flexibility. In fact, it is not difficult to find advocates who model open and pragmatic thinking, something that makes it difficult to attach strict labels to their work. For example, Dewey was a progressive in the sense that he wanted to work with children and believed in the importance of direct experience, but was a reformer as he saw the point of education was a rehearsal for the problems we face in the real world, and, if not a conservative, he took the idea of core academic knowledge seriously. Hirsch, who critics laud or dismiss as an archetypal conservative, was capable of genuine pragmatism by calling to redress the balance of the curriculum in favour of core knowledge not turning the curriculum upside down. Montessori offered an instructional role for the teacher that her critics have simply missed. This kind of flexibility is important if advocates are to inform practice for teachers themselves rarely fit into liberal, progressive, radical or conservative boxes. They adapt to the particular students in front of them and what they are expected to teach; teaching, as with leadership earlier, is 'contextual'. This often means that teaching ends up as a process of letting go, but only when it feels right to do so.

SUMMARY

In this chapter we have looked at the idea of advocacy in social research and explained six broad positions: neoliberalism with its concern for markets in education, conservatism and the importance of core knowledge; liberalism and its promotion of dialogue and reasoning; reformism, which addresses the problem that most children are bored most of the time; progressivism and the desire to see the natural unfolding of the child's understanding of the world; radicalism, which seeks to address imbalances in power. We looked at the pros and cons of each position. We discussed the value of advocacy in showing how education debates are underpinned by deeply held educational values, but argued for more pragmatic thinking about education. This is something to be pursued in our final chapter.

FURTHER READING (AND VIEWING)

As regards the ideas set out in this chapter, there are great many articles easily accessible on the functioning of Charter schools in US education. On our reading they do not seem, in terms of testable learning outcomes, to have made much difference one way or another, but that is for you to decide. The debate needs, of course, to go much wider and there is a host of literature debating the wider merits and drawbacks of neoliberalism in education. Savage's (2017) chapter *Neoliberalism, Education and Curriculum* moves us away from USA to education in Australia and gives a good overview of neoliberalism as an idea. The case for the market in low cost schools is made by Tooley and Dixon earlier.

On conservatism, Hirsch's *The Schools We Need* is one of the most accessible places to start. On liberalism, we know that putting Dewey down as a liberal thinker will upset some people, but we wanted to stress his commitment to consensus based on rational conversation. Alan Ryan's (1995) biography *John Dewey and the High Tide of American Liberalism* gives a broad introduction to Dewey and helps readers see Dewey's ideas in the context of a rapidly changing USA.

Fullan and Langworthy (2013) referenced earlier make the case for reform in the booklet *Towards a New End: New pedagogies for deep learning*. Freire's ideas are covered in his much-cited *Pedagogy of the Oppressed* (1972).

There are good short guides to progressive thinkers within the infed website *What is informal education?* (Accessed at http://infed.org/mobi/what-is-informal-education/.) This is not-for-profit site provided by the YMCA George Williams College, London.

Having earlier referenced a couple of romanticised films of teaching and learning we address the balance by recommending a fly-on-the-wall documentary that was unexpectedly popular some years ago, *Être et Avoir* (2002) or *To Be and To Have*. The film is about a single-class village school in France, and their exceptional teacher. The film shows how difficult it is to categorise the work of a teacher. There are aspects of progressivism in his teaching as the children get outside and engage with practical activities such as cooking, sledging in the snow and going on picnics, there is liberalism in that children learn to settle disputes by talking and reasoned argument and there is quite of lot of didactic teaching of basic skills too.

7

EDUCATION RESEARCH

LOOKING BACK AND LOOKING FORWARD

Here we review the ideas and debates covered in the previous chapters in order to draw some conclusions about education research and where it might be heading. It is organised around seven questions: What has been covered?; What is education research?; Which methodology and methods are used in education research?; Who is education research for? How should we read education research? What does education research tell us?; and What are the future challenges for education research?.

WHAT HAS THE BOOK COVERED?

We began by covering research carried out by practitioners, noting the different forms this research took, and highlighted its value as offering an eclectic, context rich style of reporting. Action research comes as close as anything can to ensuring that research has an impact on practice, even though it rarely seeks to offer generalised conclusions.

We next explored a more 'scientific' approach to education, very often conducted by professional researchers, not always with a practice background. We discussed the experimental research tradition, and saw meta-analysis and systematic review as particularly useful because of their scale, and because they offered a longitudinal dimension that reduced the influence of novelty and short term impact. However, large-scale studies ran the risk of focusing on too narrow a range of learning outcomes and mistaking association for causality. This criticism extended towards PISA and we critiqued PISA's growing influence on education systems.

The challenges encountered in making large-scale generalisation led us back, in Chapter 3, to smaller scale studies, very often case studies, which offered detailed descriptions of, in one example, classroom life. Small-scale research is carried out by academic researchers, often in collaboration with practitioners, as well as by practitioners themselves. These studies can result in important guidance for practice.

In Chapter 4 we went into more detail about explanation and the kinds of explanations that education researchers put forward. We argued that a mix of approaches was needed to give a full picture of how and why something was happening. We discussed theory as having several meanings and explored one particular type of theory that aimed to be more abstract, speculative and transferable. We also saw that theories about education were developed in cross or interdisciplinary contexts and argued for a balanced relationship between education and other disciplines.

Finally, we looked at advocacy as a way of organising ideas as to what was going wrong in education and how teaching and learning could be improved. We discussed the merits of different perspectives and argued that advocates were often more flexible, and their arguments more research based, than critics allowed.

WHAT IS EDUCATION RESEARCH?

An indication of the scope of education is given in the topics covered in this book: how practitioners can improve their practice; how young people learn; the strategies teachers use for teaching and managing classrooms; the strategies students use for learning (including ways of avoiding learning); the variations in learning outcomes; how schools are managed; learning outside the classroom; how leaders lead and followers are led; the way the curriculum is organised; the assessment of learning; the nature of knowledge; the relationship between society and school; learning in dangerous contexts; individual needs and personalisation; the take-up (or non-take-up) of technology. Yet this only just touches the surface of what could have been covered. Education research is very broad area of study indeed. However, there is a unifying thread to education research. Researchers are interested in change, in particular how we go from one way of understanding the world to another. This leads us to cover questions of organisation (e.g. how schools are organised and how the curriculum is arranged); teacher and practitioner interventions (e.g. strategies, preparation of teaching, support for teachers); learner responses (e.g. learner types, strategies, intentions, theories of learning); the relationship of formal to informal learning and the relationship of both to broader society (including questions of power, access and fairness).

But were education only interested in change it could as an area of study be quite easily integrated into one or more of other subject disciplines: economics, history, literature, politics, sociology, philosophy, psychology or whatever. Of course, research in these other disciplines helps education researchers do their work: literature offers insight into intra personal thinking; history describes research traditions; psychology focuses on individual difference and individual development; politics shows how policies are made and enacted; philosophy provides precision in defining concepts such as equality, fairness, truth and warranted assertions; sociology explains the group and group activity. But what makes education research distinctive is that researchers are interested not only in change but in the quality of change, in other words how we can help learners go from one way of understanding culture, society, the physical world, etc. to a way that is better. A distinction is sometimes made between educational research, which is directly concerned with improving practice, and education research, a broad term to cover all kinds of research on education. We do not consistently use that terminology as all education research should ultimately be *for education*, it has to ask how can we can do this better, if not it ceases to be education research. All education researchers have an ingrained action orientation, and this includes those who have no truck with action research itself. What, then, makes education research distinctive is that researchers are interested not only in change but in the quality of change. Thus, we saw in Chapter 1 action researchers may ask 'How can I better engage learners?' but in Chapter 5 a sociologist may ask 'How can I theorise the anti-school behaviour of certain groups of youngsters?'.

What though is *better* in the context of education. This is of course, up for debate but better will generally mean gaining knowledge that is more valid, trustworthy, relevant, useful, practical, able to withstand the test of time, able to withstand the test of experiment, all in some combination. Quality matters a lot to educational researchers. For example in Chapter 5 we described a CoP as an environment in which members come together to create joint practices and solve problems. CoP theory gives important insight into the way groups work and the way that new members are supported in their journey to full participation. CoP has helped education researchers see the importance of learning that takes place outside of formal learning contexts. But what specifically interests education researchers is the quality of a CoP – we need to know how and why learning is better carried out in some CoPs than others. Moreover, we need to know that what is learnt in a CoP is open to critical scrutiny. Learning for educationalists involves the capacity to weigh up conflicting evidence and to reach one's own conclusions. Learning certainly involves dialogue and cooperation with others but it is not about following the crowd or believing what one is expected to believe. As we saw in discussing the liberal view of learning, it involves reflection and reflexivity.

WHICH METHODOLOGIES AND METHODS ARE TYPICAL OF EDUCATION RESEARCH?

Education research covers a broad range of approaches and many methods are used in collecting data. We argued that research questions drive methodologies and methods and this leads us to reject the idea that there is a gold standard for assessing the value or quality of research. Rather the quality of the research depends on the quality of those questions – Are they pressing? Are they relevant for the profession? Are they coherent? Are they covering new ground?

As to the research carried out, we have reported small-scale case studies that have the goal of providing in-depth understanding of particular contexts: classrooms, children's outdoor play, learning at work, learning in communities; online environments. These studies have often been concerned with understanding the stakeholder (e.g. practitioners, students, parents, leaders) perspectives using qualitative methods such as interviews, observations, diary keeping, shadowing, document analysis and open-ended surveys. At times researchers, in particular advocates, have used more impressionistic approaches such as ethnography and autoethnography too. In contrast, larger scale studies were seen as belonging to a more positivist tradition with the aim of identifying patterns, including strength of association between variables, within large sets of quantitative data.

We should, however, be careful of dividing education research into two unbreachable paradigms: interpretivism, with its qualitative methodology, and positivism, with its quantitative. Education researchers are pragmatic and will call upon a mix of methods; many are quite happy to accept that there are *things* that can be counted and described 'objectively' (though an objectivity that is always skewed to what the researcher finds of interest) and *perspectives on things* (subjective perceptions of stakeholders). Both things and perspectives on things need to be considered. Thus, much education research will end up comparing and contrasting different kinds of data.

We found in Chapter 5 that the point of education research was not just to collect the data but to explain how and why something has happened. Different kinds of explanation were discussed (Table 5.1) and the idea of theory was introduced. Education research is often accused of being under theorised but theory can mean many things and we saw that theory made a contribution when it helped to organise our thoughts about an event or practice and to focus on the essentials. We found that theories were leaps of the imagination and often emerged from research on a surprisingly small-scale.

WHO IS EDUCATION RESEARCH FOR?

The book illustrates that education research can be written for different purposes and different audiences. For example research may be written directly for practitioners (e.g. Gardiner, 2017); evaluation research may be written to give feedback on innovations, and for future planning (e.g. Banerjee et al., 2007); meta-studies and large data sets may be used in search of generalisations (Higgins, 2018); case studies may inform understanding by shining a light on what is important in an approach or intervention (Littleton et al., 2005); advocacy research may point out shortcomings and argue for change (e.g. Hirsch, 1996); and education may be a site for exploring discipline questions (e.g. Molfese et al., 2013). The audiences for such research are fairly clear: practitioners want to read practice research that will help them do their job better; policy makers want to read general research to inform the decisions they have to make; academics want to engage with conceptual exploration. These purposes and audiences are summarised in Table 7.1 – this relates closely to, but extends Table 5.1 earlier.

However, Table 7.1 only indicates the primary purposes and audiences for types of education research but different types of education research should reach across audiences. For example, research for understanding should be able to inform practice and often does so when practitioners carrying out their own accredited research projects; advocacy research appeals (or is rejected) right across the board; practice research gets academics arguing about the nature of professional knowledge and how such knowledge is obtained; generalisations about teaching directly inform practice, as seen with the idea of visible teaching. Such boundary hopping is made easier when researchers spell out the implications for practice, no matter what kind of research is being undertaken.

HOW SHOULD WE READ EDUCATION RESEARCH?

We should read education research critically and this means understanding that the researchers are fallible, as is our reading of it.

We should be aware that no matter how convincing the prescriptions or ideas we read about, they will never tell us what we need to do. We can learn from past research but our job is to reinterpret it to address the problems we face in our own classrooms, lecture halls, families, work places or wherever. When we read about Hattie's

Table 7.1 The purpose and audience for different types of education research

Type of research	Purpose	Audience	Typical questions the researcher asks
Practice research	To address problems of practice	Practitioners; academics sympathetic to or helping with action research; funders of professional development	How can I improve/address X in my work?
Evaluation research	To assess impact and inform the process of intervention (formative); to identify strengths and weaknesses and inform future decision making (summative)	Policy makers and other funding bodies	What has changed with intervention X? What opportunities and challenges have appeared? What recommendations should be made?
Education research for understanding	To describe what is happening; to build new concepts; to test old concepts	Academics	How can we capture what is happening here?

continued

Table 7.1 Continued

Type of research	Purpose	Audience	Typical questions the researcher asks
Education research for generalising	To describe general patterns with large sets of data; to identify relationships between variables	Policy makers; academics	Does X work better than Y?
Advocacy research	To show how education falls short; to raise moral questions	Academics; practitioners; general public	How can education be better organised?
Academic research based in other disciplines	To explore discipline problems using education as a context	Academics	Can we extend /illustrate discipline questions in the context of education?

visible teaching, or case studies of deep learning, or the value of outdoor play, we need to know that just because it happened in context X, this does not mean it will happen in context Y. We can relate to these studies but we need to ask ourselves questions: In what ways does this context look similar to my context, in what ways is it different? Which recommendations might cross over to my context and why? What do I need to pay special attention to? Critical distance should be applied when reading all studies. Large-scale meta-studies, seen in Chapter 2, score highly on reliability, but we should not forget that the explanations that researchers put forward are speculative. In reading meta-analyses readers need to ask critical questions: Where were the studies collected from? In what ways were these studies skewed? Has the situation changed? What conclusions can be justifiably drawn? In contrast to research on a large scale, small case studies, as well as the more impressionistic work from Holt, can be beguiling as they take us up close to the classroom or other locations being researched. But again, we need to ask critical questions: Were the contexts being described chosen as they were typical or unusual and does the researcher really know which? What has been omitted in making the account clear to us? What other interpretations might be possible?

We need to be aware that when we are reading about education, we are not making value free judgements. We cannot get rid of our prejudices and should not get rid of our values. However, our often deeply held assumptions about education may mislead us into overstating the importance of some kinds of research or failing to treat other research fairly. We need to understand the context in which research was carried out and make due allowance. For example, Pestalozzi was a progressive – to us perhaps an out and out one. But consider for a minute that one of the hallmarks of his progressivism was that he abolished flogging in his schools! In similar vein, Montessori was writing about the rights of the child at a time when Mussolini was having school children believe that they were servants of the Fascist state. How might this have affected what they wrote and what is the filter through which we read research today: Do we think schools have got it all wrong? Are researchers out of touch romantics? Are researchers tainted by commercial influences?

WHAT DOES EDUCATION RESEARCH TELL US?

We have been careful in this book to deal as fairly as possible with different views of education and different traditions of research, but is there anything we feel that education research tells us fairly incontrovertibly? Well, there are five things we feel pretty sure about:

First, education matters. Education – or at least education that meets a certain quality – can have important economic consequences for developing and developed countries (Hanushek & Woßmann, 2010; Karoui & Feki, 2018). Education can have important social consequences too and an educated public provides the basis for a civil society in which ideas are discussed and debated (Mercer, 2012). And education matters for individuals by providing economic and social opportunities (Hirsch, 2010) and the intelligent agency that enables them to identify life choices and to be able to act on those choices (Bronfenbrenner, 1979). We agree with the liberal position that anyone, or any country, that neglects the education of their children has violated the rights of the child (Ryan, 2001). Education matters as it serves society but teachers are not servants of society, they need to keep a distance. Schools and other institutions cannot do only what policy makers want them to do.

Second, a key fact of educational systems is that outcomes are differentiated and, to put this more clearly, outcomes are not fair. We should dwell on this particular finding: attainment will be skewed by factors such as class, race and gender in ways that should not be happening. We know from analysing large sets of data, collected in both national and international settings, that such outcomes are not inevitable, but it is clear that obstacles are being put in the way of some and not others. We can disagree over the cause of these obstacles but we can agree that education systems have to address them.

Third, research tells us that if we want to improve education then this cannot be achieved by top down directives from leaders and policy makers, nor can it be bottom up, reliant on the efforts of individual teachers (Fullan, 2007). All levels of a system need to work in tandem (Bronfenbrenner, 1979). For example, if trying to address the well-being of children, policy makers need to consider what in the system is stressing children; schools need to know how they deal with anti-social behaviour and whether their curriculum is leaving gaps in the way it promotes well-being; individual teachers need to work on creating positive classroom environments; parents need to know how they can support their children and provide them with opportunities to develop healthy life styles; students themselves have to change their behaviour. But no matter how far parents, schools, children, teachers are lined up in support of change, there are influences beyond education systems that affect whatever is being promoted.

Fourth, education research gives us a great deal of guidance about pedagogy that has been developed with practitioners, or by talking and watching practitioners, and shown to be useful across different contexts. For example, if not incontestable, research tells us that it is a really good idea if teachers: learn not only their subject but how to teach their subject (Shulman, 1986); expand their repertoire of skills throughout their careers (e.g. Darling-Hammond, 2010); adjust their teaching to their students (Banerjee et al., 2007); use a wide repertoire of question types (Walsh and Sattes, 2016); make expectations of group work explicit (Littleton et al., 2005); be proactive and positive in exercising control (Rogers, 2011) and so on. Some might say the conclusions about teaching that researchers provide are obvious but if they were obvious, they would have become routine. There are also a large number of things that seem equally obvious to some people but are not backed up by research evidence.

Fifth, and this is really part of our previous point, but it so important that it needs to be highlighted in its own right, formative feedback needs to be given to show students what they need to do to improve. Here the wisdom of practice, systematic review, case study and learning theory all point the same way: formative feedback, including AfL, improves learning. This is a conclusion that really does seem to cross most contexts. Formative feedback is what makes teacher questioning an opportunity for learning rather than an empty ritual, formative feedback from peers is what makes group work come alive. Formative feedback must be within the student's grasp, it is of no value to show a child how to write an essay if they are making their first steps in writing their name; feedback must be responsive and the best feedback creates a conversation about learning between student and teacher, or more knowledgeable mentor, parent, peer. Again obvious? Well, no. Education systems typically focus more on summative rather than formative learning, many practitioners are unsure how to provide such feedback and many students unsure how to act on it. Research shows how important such feedback is and ways in which it can be given.

WHAT ARE FUTURE CHALLENGES IN EDUCATION RESEARCH?

Finally, we note that there are many challenges facing education researchers today, and here we highlight six of these.

First, we need to 'get out more'. Past research has not neglected out of institutional contexts, nor disregarded informal learning in general, but more could have been done. Learning goes on everywhere: in newspapers and on television; within online forums, blogs and websites; in conversations at work, clubs and societies; in homes and outdoors in playgrounds and parks; in museums, cinemas and theatres and so on. We need to explore the quality of this learning and to show the opportunities as well as the limitations. Education researchers should not be precious when commenting on informal contexts, there is plenty of room in life for 'base pleasures' as Mill (in Chapter 6) would dismiss spontaneous feelings and immediate gratifications. But without moments in the home, workplace or in wider civil society when something more reflective, considered and open-minded goes on we will be in trouble as individuals, groups and societies. At the time of writing it seems urgent to understand and promote such moments.

Second, we should show flexibility and pragmatism. We can engage with the foundational questions in education: Whether teaching should be inductive or deductive?, What is knowledge? and What does it mean to learn? But the answers we give are rarely one size fits all. There is an argument for a balance of teaching and learning approaches and an acceptance that not only teachers will want to do things in different ways but so will students. This opens a space in which the key question to be asked is not whether one approach is better than another but whether we are seeing a good example of its kind? For example, the lesson on parts of speech described by John Holt was not good of its kind, the lesson on weather patterns was; talk in the early years classroom described by Littleton et al. was at first not good of its kind but a later instance found to be exemplary. All of us have attended lectures and found ourselves stimulated, amused and coming away knowing much more than when we went in. All of us have, too, sat through long presentations that have strained our patience to breaking point. The question is what makes the former work and the latter so unsatisfactory?

Third, we need to contribute to a more informed debate about education. In particular we need to call out where reporting or discussion of education is distorting understanding. If you follow, even for a short time, debates within social platforms and reporting in the media in general you will see examples where something becomes accepted, or at least put forward as a generalisable truth on flimsy evidence: We all have inherent learning styles; PISA is a reliable measure on how well our education system is doing; praise is not helpful; East Asian schools are better than those in the USA; Drinking more water keeps the brain hydrated; setting students by ability works; Smaller classes mean better test outcomes; Homework is the key to academic success; Schools are getting worse and so on. Some of these statements can be tracked back to a skewed reading of the research, some are pretty much made up.

Fourth, we need to challenge narrow definitions of education effectiveness. Increasingly, schools and systems are being judged on objective test outcomes, including PISA data, and national examination data, often from a narrow range of subjects. There is nothing wrong with doing this, but there is a problem when the focus on testing becomes overwhelming. There are a range of questions that education systems need to address, which cannot be answered by testing: How can well-being be promoted and widespread feelings of unhappiness be addressed?; How can community cohesion be supported in school?; how can creativity be supported in the curriculum?; How can schools help model democratic citizenship? One finding in the PISA data referred to in Chapter 3 was that parents value schools where their children are safe and happy above academic attainment. Of course, one does not rule out the other, quite the opposite in many cases, but the finding suggests that we need a wider sense of the purpose of education.

Fifth, although it has become a cliché of the modern discourse, we really do live in a fast changing global world, defined by rapid movements of capital, people and ideas. One implication here is that what happens in educational systems throughout the world should matter to us. We should understand the successes and challenges in other systems, and take to heart failings such as the lack of access to education affecting so many young people worldwide. In the face of globalisation some have called for a decolonisation of the curriculum. We need to find ways to address these demands that take students and teachers along with us, but without throwing out all that has been covered in the past – in quiet but determined ways Keane et al. (2017) do this.

Sixth, whatever challenges we face we need to remember that it is impossible to think about desirable change in education without the commitment and good will of the teacher. The continuing challenge is for education research to be written with the concerns of practitioner in mind and communicated to practitioners in accessible ways with implications for practice spelt out. Educational research is concerned with how can we make things better – in which 'what is better' is open for debate. Education research needs to speak not just to academic or policy audiences but to students, practitioners, parents or carers, volunteer teachers and organisers of voluntary associations, and an informed general public.

KEY WORDS

Abduction: often used to describe an approach to analysis that alternates between inductive and deductive methods. Abduction is more generally the process of jumping from the data, to a conclusion, explanation, theory or hypothesis. Abduction involves a 'leap of the imagination'.

Action research: a term coined by social psychologist Kurt Lewin (1890–1947). Lewin suggested the action research 'spiral' of: plan, act, observe and reflect. Action research is usually undertaken by a person who is both the researcher and practitioner/user. For example, researchers might aim to explore how and in what ways certain aspects of their teaching are 'effective'; this research could then inform and improve their current practice. Carr and Kemmis (1986) argued that all action research has the key features of improvement of practice and the involvement of practitioners in all phases, i.e. planning, acting, observing and reflecting. A consequence of action research is an improvement in the understanding practitioners have of their practice and the practice itself.

Agency: looks at the capacity of individuals to act independently and to make their own decisions. In neoliberalism agency is often but not necessarily tied to the idea of rational decision-making, based on an understanding of economic interest. Educationalists tend to have a wide view of agency; agency is not just the idea of being able to do what one likes, but intelligent agency is based on an awareness of one's situation, including what has influenced one's choices, the range of available responses, and the likely consequence of whatever decisions one makes.

Alogrithms: a process or set of rules to be followed in problem solving, used especially in computing to describe a set of instructions. For example, Facebook uses algorithms to calculate which advertisements to display in a news feed, which take account of past online behaviour.

Applied research: research directed towards solving a problem or designed to provide information that is immediately useful and applicable. Contrasted to basic research, which aims to advance knowledge and understanding, the relevance of which has still to be determined.

Attitude test: a test designed to measure a person's feelings and attitudes towards (say) social situations or people; usually seen as a relatively crude measuring instrument, often involving a Likert scale (see later).

Audiences: individuals e.g. lecturers/teachers, parents, groups or organisations (e.g. pressure groups, universities, schools) who might use the findings produced by research.

Autoethnography: a kind of qualitative research involving self-reflection on past personal experience. The idea is to draw out wider issues about education, or other areas of social research, in one's own story.

Behaviorism: in its classical form the idea that the mind is a 'blank slate' on which our sensory experiences are written – the contemporary metaphor might be a hard disk on which data are recorded. Behaviourism informs drill and practice teaching, based on continual reinforcement of correct responses. Traditionally, behaviourists conducted experiments with children in which behaviour was modified by carefully controlling a stimulus to produce a desired response. This approach became known as 'operant conditioning': if the correct response is rewarded in some way, the required behaviour can be re-enforced. Unwanted behaviour can be discouraged by punishment, though this is not as effective in shaping behaviour as the use of rewards.

Bias: the conscious or sub-conscious influence of a researcher on what and how research is carried out. Bias can/will affect: the choice of topics/problems/ questions to research; research planning and design; methods of data collection; data analysis; interpretation of results; discussion and conclusion.

Biased sample: the result of a sampling strategy that deliberately includes or excludes certain individuals or groups. A sample may be biased for good reasons (see purposive sampling).

Big Data: data have been big for many years but the term Big Data draws attention to the fact that we have more data (volume), more kinds of data (variety) and data that can be more quickly assembled and indeed continually updated (velocity). A key attribute of Big Data is that it is online; for example, education researchers may look at Twitter messages about education policy and identify how discussion have changed over time and what is of interest (or trending) right now.

Case study: the study of single 'cases' or 'units of analysis', e.g. a person, an event, a group, an organisation, a classroom, a town, a family. Commonly used in law, medicine and education. Case study researchers should continually ask: 'what is this a case of?' Case study is often chosen to explore 'how' or 'why' questions; it examines situations in their natural setting (thus achieving ecological validity) when the researcher is not attempting to control or intervene in them. Cases are often chosen to seek explanations or deepen understanding of an event, a problem, or an issue. A variety (a mix) of methods may be used to explore the 'case' from different angles and perspectives (see triangulation).

Causality: the process of a cause producing an effect; the general public and perhaps some researchers often seek causality – we seem to have a natural tendency to search for the causes of things. But we can rarely see, let alone prove, causality clearly or with certainty. There may often be associations between events and even correlations but this is not the same as causality. Some philosophers (such as David Hume) argued that there is no such thing as causality between one event and another – Hume suggested that there is simply 'constant conjunction' between them. For example, poverty might be a good 'predictor' of low educational achievement (though few would say it **causes** low achievement). The search for and belief in direct causality, i.e. X causes Y, is now highly debatable in modern science and in education research.

Coding: this involves attaching names or labels to an idea (or unit of meaning) within an interview or observation notes. It is a way of reducing masses of data into manageable categories. Using codes researchers can highlight patterns and make relevant comparisons across different data, e.g. a set of interviews. In generating codes, the researcher has a choice between top down (deductive) or bottom up (inductive) approaches – in practice there might be a great deal of initial work before a coding schema can be settled.

Cognition: the act of knowing or understanding; knowledge can be knowledge that or knowledge how and in some cases knowledge why. Thus, the process of cognition can involve skill, knowledge or understanding. The cognitive domain of thought is often distinguished from the affective domain, which concerns emotion, attitude and feeling. Both domains have been the focus of education research.

Constructionism: is often used in social research to offer a view that our minds are not blank slates but rather we are meaning makers. 'Radical constructivism' argues that there is no reality, only our perception of it. This is a concept that is hard to swallow when you walk into a lamppost. The radical constructivist might argue that there is no such thing as 'truth' or facts – in the current era, this would lead to discussion of how 'fake news' differs from 'real' news.

Constructivism: a learning theory that all knowledge is constructed. Piaget, for example, suggested that knowledge is gained by a process of assimilation ('taking in' new experiences) and accommodation (modifying our conceptual apparatus to make sense of them).

Control group: the group of people (or plants or animals) in an experiment who do not experience the treatment given to an experimental group – ideally, the control group should be as identical as possible to the experimental group. In theory, the purpose of a control group is to show what would have happened to the experimental group if it had not been exposed to the experimental treatment.

Correlation: a connection or association between two events. A correlation between two events or phenomena is not to be confused with a causal connection. For example, it has been said that economic recession is correlated with a rise in thefts from property but the causal connection is not clear. In complex, real life events there are often 'confounding variables' i.e. variables in a situation that we are not aware of or we have ignored.

Curriculum: what is taught and how it is taught within a school or programme of study. A subject curriculum generally covers the knowledge and skills to be covered and the associated assessment. Extra-curricular refers to experiences outside of formal teaching – for example organised sports, field trips, educational visits, the word extra here signifying outside or beyond. The hidden curriculum covers what is not explicitly taught but rather the underlying expectations about teaching and learning, and particularly about conduct, in school. For example, a goal of the hidden curriculum may be to develop moral understanding, a sense of social compassion or an acceptance of privilege and authority, depending on your viewpoint.

Deconstruction: a way of examining texts by 'taking them apart', often used in the sense of searching for the unspoken or unformulated messages of a text, i.e. the text can be shown to be saying something more than or different to what it appears or purports to say. There is not one essential meaning of text. Documentary analysis often involves deconstruction.

Deductive: the deductive method in philosophy is about drawing valid conclusions from initial premises. It follows the logic of syllogy expressed in classical form as:

Socrates is a man (major premise)
All men are mortal (minor premise)
Therefore Socrates is mortal (conclusion)

When applied to social research it has been associated with the hypothetico-deductive approach. This involves setting out specific hypotheses for inquiry based on past research. The hypothesis is then tested under experimental conditions, perhaps a randomised control trial. If the data support the hypothesis then the hypothesis is shown as valid, at least in that context. This is a cyclical process, hypotheses are continually put forward, their validity assessed. In teaching and learning a deductive method usually consists in a top down instructional strategy: the teacher sets out the principles of a topic, or a way of looking at a topic, and pupils practice these principles in a controlled setting. Following the logic of the hypothetical deductive method students can critically examine the validity of those principles, although this is often underdeveloped in top down instructional teaching.

Dependent variable: the thing/phenomenon that you study or measure in a controlled experiment; it is the variable changed or influenced by an experimental treatment.

Description: an account of what is happening or what has happened. Description is easily underrated. The researcher needs to exercise skill and discretion when deciding what to include in a description and how to structure that description. There is an important distinction to be made between *thin* and *thick* description. Thick description seeks to provide a detailed account of an aspect of human behaviour through reference to the context in which it takes place; thin description describes the act, the thick description deals with meaning of the act.

Discipline: an academic discipline defines a domain of knowledge. A discipline sets up boundaries as to: what is studied; what are expected ways of conducting a study; by what criteria can new knowledge be admitted into a discipline and old knowledge discarded (see Paradigm). A discipline also describes institutional arrangements, for example higher education is divided into disciplines with specialist staff and dedicated infrastructure. Disciplines enable knowledge to be constructed in coherent and focused ways so that discipline knowledge can develop over time. However, discipline boundaries can be criticised as arbitrary and restricting, i.e. there to keep others out. Thus, increasing interest in interdisciplinary, crossdisciplinary, and transdisciplinary approaches.

Discourse analysis: a general term used to encompass a range of approaches to analysing talk, text, writing etc.; mainly concerned with examining and deconstructing **what** is being communicated and **how, by** looking for codes, rules and signs in speech or text.

Document analysis: the strategies and procedures for analysing and interpreting the documents of any kind that might be important for the study of a particular area. Documents might be public, e.g. government documents, media cuttings, television scripts, minutes of meetings; or private, e.g. letters, diaries, school records, memoirs, interview transcripts, transcripts prepared from video records or photographs. The analysis should consider: the context of the document; its sub-text (what lies beneath it); its pre-text (what has gone before it); and its inter-text (how it relates to other documents).

Ecological validity: the idea that a study is more 'valid' if it explores an event or a phenomenon e.g. classroom talk, a child's language, lecturing styles, in its natural setting as opposed to in an observation room, a clinic or a lab. A truly ecological study takes account of the immediate context (the micro), the slightly broader and related contexts (the meso) and the national or global context (the macro). As an aside, the term 'validity' is itself problematic in that it is used in many different ways by researchers.

Educational research: this covers inquiry into every aspect of education and learning. Empirical education research uses a variety of methods: qualitative, quantitative and mixed. Education research draws upon a variety of disciplines including: history because of what the past educational approaches can tell us; psychology because of its focus on the individual difference and individual development; politics because of its focus on the way policies are made and enacted; philosophy for its precision in defining concepts such as equality, fairness, truth and warranted assertions; sociology because of its focus on the group and group processes. Education research is particularly interested in how systems of education can be improved. A distinction is sometimes made between **educational** research, which is directly concerned with improving practice, and **education** research, a broad term to cover all kinds of research on education.

Effect sizes: this is a measure of how effective an intervention or treatment turns out to be after a study or a trial (see RCT). Effect size tells us the magnitude of the difference between groups. It should be used alongside p-values, which tell us the significance of the support or evidence for a hypothesis about those groups.

Empirical research: (as opposed to deskwork or 'armchair' research) is inquiry involving first-hand data collection, e.g. interviewing, observing, surveying. People can do empirical research without being 'empiricist'.

Empiricism: the belief that all reliable knowledge is dependent upon and derived from sensory experience – see the Scottish philosopher David Hume (1711–76). The strict form of empiricism is logical positivism, which maintains that the only valid knowledge claims are those that are directly verifiable by sense data. This rules out most social science, the bulk of modem science (including physics), all of theology and metaphysics, ethics and morals, and most theory of any kind. A bit too strict, perhaps, and widely attacked, e.g. by Kuhn, Polanyi, and later Wittgenstein.

Enlightenment: generally refers to ideas from leading intellectuals in Western Europe in the eighteenth and nineteenth centuries who, inspired by advances in natural science, wanted to explain the social world in more scientific ways. This led them to critique political and social arrangements based on superstition or tradition; all such arrangements should be based on reason. Key intellectual figures included Adam Smith, David Hume in Scotland, Immanuel Kant in Prussia and French figures such as Voltaire and Montesquieu. By exercising reason, we become better, fuller human beings, while at a social level we can have a rule of law and a democratic public sphere. In terms of method this led to a concern for experiment and observation and tolerance for opposing views.

Epistemology: this is the study of how we know things i.e. the nature and validity of human knowledge or 'episteme' in Greek. It often (e.g. in Plato's work) examines the difference between knowledge and belief. The two traditional camps have been: rationalism, which stresses the role of human reason in knowing;

and empiricism, which stresses the importance of sensory perception. Immanuel Kant argued that most knowledge is a synthesis or combination of the two approaches. Roughly, perceptions without concepts are blind, concepts without perceptions are empty (this sounds better in German).

Ethical guidelines: a set of rules or moral guidelines, which should be followed in planning, conducting and writing up research. These may vary slightly from one organisation to another but most of us would not involve people in research without their full consent or try to force or pressure anyone into doing anything against their will e.g. having an interview recorded. We would as a rule keep all participants fully informed about the research and what they are 'letting themselves in for'; confidentiality and anonymity should be maintained at all stages. Above all, researchers should seek to 'do no harm'.

Ethnography: a methodology with its roots in anthropology (literally, the study of people); it aims to describe and interpret human behaviour within a certain culture; uses extensive fieldwork and participant observation, aiming to develop rapport and empathy with people studied.

Experimental group: the group of people in a controlled experiment who experience the experimental treatment or intervention.

Explanation: offers a reason why something has happened and is often contrasted with description (an account of what happened) though the distinction is a matter of degree, not kind. A positivist explanation is more likely to be confident in identifying cause and effect, may well use statistical testing of some kind, and see validity and reliability as 'warrants' of its quality. Causality is treated with caution within interpretive approaches as researchers often seek to make activity comprehensible, and to show the consequences of action, rather than to speculate on cause and effect.

External validity: is the extent to which the findings or conclusions of a piece of research could be generalised to apply to contexts/ situations other than those in which the data have been collected.

Fine-grained: grain is the pattern of fibres within a wood and a fine-grained texture is one that is smooth – this can be contrasted to course-grained wood, which is rough to the touch. These terms are transferred across to social research so that a fine-grained analysis leaves no rough edges, it takes in everything. In contrast a coarse-grained analysis might focus on the key factors in a study. Fine-grained sounds better but it is not necessarily so. Researchers need to balance how closely they represent a case (the fidelity) with transferability (which is made easier when a small number of key variables are highlighted).

Focus groups: a research method, similar to interviewing, but involving a small group of people in a discussion on a certain issue or problem. Its advantage is that group members can stimulate or spark off each other's thoughts and lead to a richer set of research data. Its drawback is that not everyone likes to speak when part of a group and certain 'maverick voices' may dominate if allowed to. Like interviews, focus groups can range from unstructured to semi to highly structured.

Forest School Movement: a broad movement united around a concern that children are missing out on outdoor activities. In many forest school initiatives children are encouraged to engage in problem solving activities with the aim of developing confidence in working together. Physical work is encouraged, e.g. preparing food and eating it together. Conventional schools are seen as too sanitised.

Formal learning: refers to the learning that goes on in organised events such as timetable classes, in-service training days, online courses. Formal learning is explicit, structured and often described as intentional. Formal learning leads to certification. In contrast informal learning is much more serendipitous. It goes on at work, in the community or in the spaces between classrooms. It usually is triggered by encounters with others but might consist of personal reflection on experiences and events. The definition seems watertight but we can learn informally in formal contexts − for example by striking up conversations with others in the course of an in-service session − and quite formally in informal sessions − for example a chat about how to do something at work may lead to some quite explicit mentoring or coaching.

Formative assessment/evaluation: assessment or evaluation carried out in the early or intermediate stages of a programme, a course or an intervention while changes can still be made; the formative evaluation shapes and informs those changes. Summative assessment or evaluation is carried out at the end of a programme or intervention to assess its impact. Formative assessment and feedback is part of assessment for learning (AfL).

Generalisability: the extent to which research findings in one context can be transferred or applied to other contexts or settings. No findings can be generalised with complete certainty. Often used alongside transferability. Can be contrasted with relatability – the idea that the reader can see enough in a description of a study to be able to say how it looks similar or different from their own context. Relatability highlights the importance of adaption rather than adoption.

Grounded theory: theory 'emerging' from the data collected in a research study by the process of induction. This has the benefit of often producing new/original theory, which can later be tested by another researcher. However, there are problems, for example over the idea of 'emerging' in that theories must 'emerge' from somewhere (i.e. the researcher) and therefore must be open to testing and question.

Hawthorne effect: initial improvement in performance following any newly introduced change – an effect or problem that researchers need to be wary of when making an intervention into a natural setting, e.g. introducing new teaching methods to assess their impact. The name is based on a 1924 study of productivity at the Hawthorne factory in Chicago. Two carefully matched groups (experimental and control) were isolated from other factory workers. Factors in the working conditions of the experimental group were varied, e.g. illumination, humidity, temperature, rest periods. No matter what changes were made, including negative ones such as reduced illumination or shorter rest periods, their productivity showed an upward trend. Just as surprisingly, although no changes were made to the conditions of the control group, their output increased steadily.

Hermeneutics: the art or science of interpretation, a term first coined by William Dilthey (1833–1911). The term may now apply to the interpretation of a text, a work of art, human behaviour, discourse, documents and so on. Hans–Georg

Gadamer (1900–78) proposed hermeneutics as a form of practical philosophy or methodology; the aim is to interpret and understand the meaning of social actions and social settings (including documents).

Holistic: the idea in social science you must present the whole picture, as the different parts of systems all fit together. In education a holistic approach tries to address the whole person, including questions of purpose and identity, not just cognitive goals.

Home schooling (or home education): typically a parent or carer, possibly a tutor, teaching children at home, i.e. the child does not attend school. The home school curriculum may be unstructured or structured, i.e. following the school curriculum more or less. Education is largely home based but may be supplemented by cooperation with other home schoolers and voluntary organisations. In some systems home schooling is accepted in others it is restricted. Home schooling appeals as a point of principle to some parents – they see school as oppressive or unable to promote beliefs that are important to them. In other cases, home schooling is a reaction to the particular difficulties a child experiences in school, for example bullying.

Hypothesis: a tentative proposal or unproved theory, put forward for examination and testing; it can be used to guide and direct research along certain lines with certain procedures to 'put the hypothesis to the test'.

Induction: the process of inferring a general law from the observation of particular instances. David Hume (1711–76) talked of the 'fallacy of induction': we can never be certain of a general law, e.g. 'All swans are white', based on particular observations, e.g. seeing numerous white swans. A black one is sure to appear one day. In teaching and learning, an inductive approach gives students an opportunity to draw their own conclusions based on what they have observed – for example, in Lave (1991) apprentice tailors grasped general principles of mathematics by solving practical problems.

Instrument: any technique or tool that a researcher uses, e.g. a questionnaire, an interview schedule, observation framework etc.

Interpretative approach: argues that human behaviour can only be explained by referring to the subjective states of the people acting in it; this approach can be applied to the study of social actions/ activity and texts or documents; opposed to positivism, which claims that social life can only be explained by the examination of observable entities (see empiricism).

Interviews and interview schedules: a schedule is a set of questions used in interviewing; questions may range from **closed to open**, in which respondents express their views and experiences openly and freely. Interviews may range from unstructured to semi-structured to completely structured (a face-to-face questionnaire), i.e. from totally open to completely pre-determined. Interviews are a widely used method in qualitative research and in our own experience a fascinating way of probing an issue or a problem (see also focus groups).

Knowledge: academic knowledge has traditionally been seen as exploring concepts, their meanings and their relationships to one another. Academic knowledge need not be practical but once established as true it can find an application. Using a distinction offered by Ryle (1949) academic or propositional knowledge (knowing that) can be contrasted with practical knowledge (know how). To some, academia has been too ready to dismiss know how and has failed to recognise the artistry behind professional practice (Schön, 1983). Teachers call on different kinds of knowledge and the relationship between knowing that and know how underlies many of the debates in education research. Knowledge is increasingly seen as personal, rather than impersonal; knowledge and beliefs are so closely entwined, that there is no easy distinction between what we know and what we believe (Dewey, 1930).

Learning platforms: software that allows teachers and students to access a large number of teaching resources in different formats; communicate (teacher to student, student to student, teacher to teacher); set and take online tests with automatic feedback; keep records associated with teaching and learning. Also called Virtual Learning Environments.

Learning theory: explanations about how students learn, e.g. how they come to understand, retain and use knowledge. Learning theory was dominated, in chronological order, by behaviourism; constructivism and social constructivism. Perspectives on learning theory are at present more broad based and eclectic.

Likert scales: scales often used in questionnaires to gauge a person's attitude to something; often have five possibilities ranging from strongly agree to strongly disagree. They need to be handled with care especially when trying to quantify the results coming from them and carrying out numerical analysis.

Literature review: gives an overview of what has been written about a particular field or topic: what has been said, who has said it, and prevailing theories and methodologies. Academic literature covers peer reviewed journal articles and books while professional literature is written for the profession, for example professional association and government reporting for teachers. Increasingly referred to as 'grey literature' written for 'crossover' audiences, for example evaluations of projects that carry wider significance. A literature review is sometimes divided into conceptual and empirical sections. A conceptual review might cover the history and different meaning given to key terms in the study, say participation, learning, assessment and so on. An empirical review covers what can be learnt from case studies. A systematic review follows explicit, pre-determined criteria for which studies are included and follows closely defined protocols for analysis and reporting.

Logical positivism: a philosophy developed between 1922 and 1940 by the 'Vienna Circle' based on the earlier philosophies of Augusta Comte (1798–1857) and the empiricist David Hume (1711–76); argues that the only meaningful knowledge is that based on, and verifiable by, direct sense experience. Hence, any descriptive statement that cannot be empirically verified by sense observation is meaningless. This doctrine would rule out theology, metaphysics and hermeneutics. Logical positivism is now largely discredited but is often (wrongly) confused with positivism and with 'being scientific'.

Longitudinal research: research in which data are collected and analysed from the same individuals or same organisations at different points over an extended period of time. For example, a study of a carefully chosen sample of children/youths/adults at the ages of 7, 14, 21, 28, 35, 42 – see Michael Apted's (1999) *7-UP* (London: Heinemann) and related television programmes.

Meta-analysis: a kind of systematic review, which seeks to aggregate findings often from quantitative studies. Meta-analyses might result in explicit modelling.

Method: the means through which data are gathered and analysed within a research study. Hence research methods include interviewing, surveying, observing as well as analytical tools such as content analysis, discourse analysis and inferential statistics. Methods are often discussed as quantitative or qualitative. Quantitative methods are generally seen as dealing with the collecting and measuring of data in countable form, for example test scores, Likert scales, reaction times and so on. Qualitative data may consist of words and pictures.

Methodology: generally refers to the rationale for the application of particular research methods. Methodological decisions are consequences of particular research questions. For example: 'how many' type questions suggest a survey methodology; 'how can I improve X 'questions suggest action research as a methodology; 'is this approach better than that' suggests an experimental design.

Mixed methods: refers to the use of more than one method of data collection within a single study, for example interviews + observation; survey + interviews + document analysis. As an approach, it is often broken down by concurrent or sequential collection and analysis i.e. are the methods being used, and data analysed, more or less at the same time (concurrent) or does one follow the other (sequential). The mix of methods may be equal or 'dominant', e.g. is it really a survey (dominant) with a handful of short interviews. Mixed methods are seen as providing confirming, complementary and contrasting sources of data and provide a way of bridging the gap between out-dated positivist (quantitative) and interpretivist (qualitative) paradigms.

Models and modelling: a model is a conceptual tool that serves for abstracting the important elements in a study and shows how these elements fit together. A good metaphor for a model is a map of the underground. This puts in what people need to know (connections and lines) and leaves out what they do not need (e.g. roads, railway lines, precise distances, names of shops and pubs). It is exceptionally easy to follow a tube map and difficult to plan your journey without one. In social research there are analytical models and sensitising ones, the former seeks to explain why something happens and to offer a degree of prediction, as against a sensitising model that is inviting us to view the situation in a particular way. Statistical models often appear impressive as supported by correlational measures but have been critiqued for paying too much attention to association and less to explanation.

N: the number of people or subjects studied or sampled in a research project; e.g. $N = 1$, signifies a single case study.

Narrative: a narrative has, at its core, an attempt to 'fit a story into a plot line'. Narrative enquiry may be as concerned with the form of narration as much as the content and storytelling may be considered as a 'performance' or a kind of discourse. Narrative enquiry is often reported in an accessible form and has broad popular appeal, for example being a staple component of print and broadcast journalism.

Naturalistic inquiry: a research approach that studies or observes events in their natural or everyday setting (see ecological validity).

Objective: an adjective often applied to describe a view, a belief or even an opinion. In this case it should be placed in 'scare quotes' as no belief or view could possibly be 'objective' since it comes from a person or an organisation. It must therefore be subjective. The adjective is better used to denote objective data. This signals that the data are often in the form of logged data e.g. number of questions asked; length of wait time (objective) versus perception of wait time (subjective). Objective is always a problematic word but objective data are based on events rather than perception of events.

Observation: a valuable research method for studying an issue, a problem or a phenomenon. It has yielded valuable and practical insights into classroom practices, for example wait times. Observation can range from un-structured to semi-structured to tightly structure. Observations of events in their natural setting e.g. a real lecture theatre or a school classroom, are said to have greater ecological validity than observations of artificial or unnatural contexts such as a clinic or a lab.

Ontology: the study or theory of 'what is', i.e. the characteristics of reality, the nature of things that we claim to exist. For example, if someone believes in 'royal blood' then the epistemological question is 'how do you know?', while the ontological question is 'what is the nature of royal blood?'.

p-values: a p-value measures the strength of the evidence in support of a hypothesis. In hypothesis testing we start with a 'null' hypothesis that is put to the test in some way ('null' can be seen as short for 'nullifiable' or testable). p values range from 0 to 1. After an intervention or a test, if a p-value is small (less than or equal to 0.05) then there is strong evidence against the null hypothesis so it should be rejected; if the p-value is higher, then you cannot reject the null hypothesis. (see also effect sizes)

Paradigm: a term that became fashionable following Thomas Kuhn's (1922–96) book *The Structure of Scientific Revolutions*; now commonly over-used to mean perspective/view of the world, methodological position, viewpoint, community of researchers, cognitive framework, and so on. In education research, people often speak of 'the qualitative and quantitative paradigms', as if they were separate and mutually exclusive; or the 'positivist paradigm' as if this was dogmatically held.

Participant observation: a methodology or practice with its roots in early twentieth-century anthropology and now ethnography; it entails a researcher spending a prolonged period of time participating in the daily activities of a community or a group, e.g. a tribe, a gang, a school, the armed forces; and observing their practices, norms, customs and behaviour (either overtly or covertly). In a genuine ethnography the researcher becomes socialised into the group being studied. A fine line must then be drawn between empathy and rapport with the group and over-familiarity/ total involvement. As a method it may lead to both practical concerns, e.g. safety; and ethical concerns, e.g. pretending to be something you are not, in some situations.

Personal knowledge: knowledge held by a person which is often said to be 'tacit' or informal in the sense that they know it but cannot put it into words i.e. they cannot articulate it as we can with formal knowledge. The idea is connected with intuition, 'gut feeling' or 6th sense. It also relates to the notion of situated cognition i.e. knowledge that works in one context only.

Positionality: refers to the steps taken by researchers to explain their 'position' in relation to their study, in other words how the study might be affected by their own particular background, beliefs and values. For example, educational research is carried out by researchers who were once at school themselves and come with intuitive beliefs and emotional responses to schooling. Positionality is always important but it becomes a more debated and sensitive issue when there is a greater asymmetry between the researcher and the researched, for example between an adult and a child.

Positivism: the belief that all true knowledge is based on observable phenomena (Auguste Comte, 1798–1857) (see also empiricism: all concepts are derived from experience). The term positivist is often used to describe a research project that strives to use the methods of natural science in educational research or in social science, in particular by searching for cause and effect, and in modelling of research findings or data. It is hence contrasted with interpretivism, which takes the world as capable of multiple interpretations and seeks to uncover the meaning that human beings invest in social activity. In methodology, positivism often leads to large-scale casing, meta-analyses, deductive and experimental hypothesis testing. Positivists are more likely to speak confidently of the existence of a reliable knowledge base to inform educational practice.

Pragmatism: this generates solutions that are 'fit for purpose', their validity tested by the consequences of following specific actions. Early pragmatists saw practice and theory as entwined: theory emerged from practice and could then be applied back to practice to create 'intelligent practice'. This is sometimes referred to as an abductive approach, neither induction nor deduction, but a constant process of generating and testing hypotheses. While pragmatism is strongly associated with action research, particularly drawing on Dewey (1930), a pragmatic approach is not confined to action research and has been used more generally to refer to a mixed and flexible research strategy.

Purposive/purposeful sampling: sampling done with deliberate aims in mind as opposed to a random sample or one chosen purely for its convenience and accessibility. Cases or sites may be chosen purposefully for a variety of reasons, e.g. for being typical or extreme or deviant or unique or exemplary or revelatory Thus cases or sites are selected with certain criteria in mind.

Qualitative: of or relating to quality or kind ('qualis' in Greek); adjective describing methods or approaches that deal with non-numeric data, i.e. words rather than numbers. Methods such as interviews, focus groups, observation are often seen as 'qualitative' though there is no reason why they should not involve numbers.

Quantitative: of quantity or number; methods or approaches that deal with numeric data, amounts or measurable quantities, i.e. numbers. A false dichotomy is often drawn between a qualitative and a quantitative 'paradigm', as if the two approaches could not be used to complement and enrich each other. Also, the use of quantitative data is often (wrongly) labelled 'positivism'.

Random sample: sample of the members of a given population drawn in such a way that every member of that population has an equal chance of being selected, e.g. every tenth name in a long list. Random sampling should eliminate the operation of bias in selecting a sample. The term 'population' means the entire group from which the sample is selected, e.g. every student in a particular school/college. The population itself depends on the focus and scope of the research.

Randomised controlled trial: this is said by some to be the 'gold standard' in education research. An RCT aims to test the effectiveness of a treatment or an intervention. A number of 'similar' people are recruited to take part in the trial (not an easy thing in itself). Participants are then randomly assigned (to reduce selection bias) to either an experimental group or a control group. The experimental group receives the treatment or intervention e.g. a teaching method, while the comparison or control group does not. This difference in 'treatment' lasts for the duration of the project. Both groups are closely followed for the duration and at the end the outcomes are tested or measured. The trial is then said to test the effectiveness of the intervention. RCTs seem to be a robust and fair way of 'testing' an intervention but they are not without problems: how long should the treatment last for it to be effective? Are the control and experimental groups similar or matched in every respect? Are the numbers in the trial sufficient to enable conclusions to be drawn? What is the test at the end of the RCT actually measuring and is this a worthwhile educational aim?

Reflective practice: any practice that is based on reflection i.e. pondering on what has been done, how and why. Sometimes separated into 'reflection in action' (on the hoof) and 'reflection on action' (after the event).

Reflexivity: introspection and self-examination, i.e. the act of reflecting upon and evaluating one's own impact on the situation being studied; also involves researchers in examining their own assumptions, prior experience and bias in conducting the research and analysing its findings. Reflexivity is about the researcher. The term 'reflectivity' is a wider term meaning reflection on the whole process of research.

Reliability: commonly used to describe a test or examination. The term is also used in connection with research methods in order to estimate the degree of confidence in the data. Reliability refers to the extent to which a test or technique functions consistently and accurately by yielding the same results at different times or when used by different researchers. Research is said to be reliable if it can be repeated or replicated by another researcher and/ or at a different time. In a reliable survey, questions that address similar themes should be answered in a consistent way. In relation to coding and the use of observation schedules, inter-rater moderation assists and assesses reliability. The search for reliability underpins the arguments for triangulation.

Research design: is concerned with turning a research question, a hypothesis or even a hunch or idea into a manageable project. The design process will generally include: the initial formulation of the research questions to explore; a consideration of what kind of data are to be collected and how they are to be collected (i.e. methodology and methods); planning and reflecting on the sample (if the study is to be an empirical one) and the access and ethical issues involved with this sample; deciding how the proposed data are to be analysed; and considering how the research is to be presented and disseminated. Research design provides the link between a general idea and the day to day, or week by week, planning with its associated time lines. By way of analogy an architect **designs** a new building and the clerk of works carries out the detailed **planning** and implementation.

Research diary: the record that a researcher should keep during the course of a research study or project; this might include any combination of a notebook, an audio file, video records, photographs or a computer file. A research diary may contain formal field notes, informal notes, observations and thoughts, reflections, dates and times or any other notes, images or videos relevant to a study. Ethical guidelines (discussed earlier) should be followed in keeping a research diary whatever the medium used. Participants in a research study are often asked if they could fill in a diary in which they log the events the researcher is interested in. This is a participant diary.

Sample: the smaller number of people, cases, units or sites selected from a much larger population. Some samples are assumed to be representative of the entire population, i.e. generalisable from, but this can never be done with certainty. Samples may be completely random e.g. choosing every fifth name from a long list of potential participants; a sample may be purposive i.e. deliberately chosen to include certain people (sometimes for convenience); or stratified whereby the sample includes participants from carefully chosen groups or strata e.g. from different social classes, regions or ethnicities. Within each stratum, the final sample could then be randomly or purposively selected.

Secondary data analysis: refers to analysis of data generated within other studies and made available to the wider research community. A large number of data sets are available. The main benefit of secondary data analysis is obvious: it saves you, the researcher, the time and expense of collecting data for yourself. This can be particularly important when researching sensitive topics and/or hard-to-reach populations. Secondary data analysis has been carried out in many contexts.

Shadowing: this involves following a research participant as they carry out their daily activities, for example a student or a teacher in a school can be shadowed as they go from class to class. Shadowing gives an opportunity to see what is happening not just what people say is happening and allows informal conversation during the events themselves or immediately afterwards. The research needs to establish a great deal of trust and acceptance to shadow and there are ethical boundaries on what is possible. Shadowing can take place over any appropriate length of time.

Social constructivism: in the context of learning theory this signals an interest in the social context in which we construct meaning. For Vygotsky the learner crosses a 'zone of proximal development': the difference between what is known and what, with the help of a knowledgeable other can be learnt. However, new knowledge only becomes owned when it is internalised and used in new contexts. Vygotsky put an emphasis on rehearsal of ideas, for example we use inner speech to work out how ideas fit together and Vygotsky saw play as an important part of child development as it allowed the creative use of new concepts.

Statistics: descriptive statistics are used to describe the basic features of the data in a survey. They provide simple summaries in figures and in graphical displays. Typically, descriptive reporting includes the distribution of responses either in raw totals (percentages or numbers) or as grouped by age ranges, gender, ethnicity or other criteria. Other descriptive reporting includes the central tendency (the mean, median and mode) and the dispersion (the standard deviation). At a more sophisticated level researchers may employ inferential statistics, tests that go beyond the immediate data, to infer likely associations between variables. The key principle within inferential statistics is that a comparison is made between the data as collected and the data as they would be if distributed 'by chance'.

Stimulated recall: a method used with research participants to help jog their memory or spark off some thoughts about an event or an incident e.g. a lecture, a lesson, past memories of education. An image, a video or even a spoken reminder can act as the stimulus for a research participant to recall and perhaps discuss the event or experience that is relevant to the research study. Stimulated recall can be used in an interview but often works well with a focus group in which the stimulus e.g. a piece of video may help members to recall and then discuss a shared experience.

Structures: refer to the ways in which society is organised (i.e. the distribution of wealth but also the functioning of social institutions and the nature of cultural expectations) and the effect this organisation has on the individual.

Theory: theories set out to explain a social or physical phenomenon or event; a theory may take different forms, e.g. an idea, a model or a principle. The common thread is that theory is used to explain why things happen as they do. Theory seeks patterns, relationships, correlations, associations or connections, e.g. between aspects of behaviour and factors that might affect it or explain it. Some theories may be predictive but they might also offer a more general picture as to how data fit together. Theorising might also consist of applying concepts to new data and developing new concepts taking account of observations and previous concepts. Theory can also be normative (what ought to happen) and can have a meta-dimension so that theorising can be thinking about theory and those who propose theoretical frameworks.

Triangulation: the business of giving strength or support to findings/ conclusions by drawing on evidence from other sources: (i) other methods (methodological triangulation), e.g. interviews, observations, questionnaires; (ii) other researchers; (iii) other times, e.g. later in a project; (iv) other places, e.g. different regions.

Trustworthiness: a criterion offered by Lincoln and Guba (1985) as an alternative to the traditional 'reliability' and 'validity' in judging research. Trustworthiness has four parts: (i) credibility; (ii) transferability (cf. external validity); (iii) dependability; (iv) confirmability (the latter two being parallel to reliability).

Validity: the extent or degree to which an inquiry, a method, test, technique or instrument measures what it sets out or purports to measure, e.g. an intelligence test, an interview, a questionnaire. No instrument could ever be said to be valid with total certainty. Validity can be seen as a measure of the confidence in, credibility of, or plausibility of a piece of research. In quantitative research often shown via measurement.

Variable: a measurable or non–measurable characteristic, which varies from one individual or organisation to another. Some may be qualitative, in say the form of words and pictures, others quantitative, i.e. expressible as numbers. Age, gender, ability, personality characteristics, 'intelligence' are a few examples of human variables. In some approaches, the researcher attempts to control or manipulate variables; in other approaches, the researcher studies or observes them in their natural setting.

REFERENCES

Arendt, H. (1961/1977). *Between Past and Present*. London: Penguin.

Banerjee, A. V., Cole, S., Duflo, E., & Linden, L. (2007). Remedying education: Evidence from two randomized experiments in India. *The Quarterly Journal of Economics, 122*(3), 1235–1264.

Biesta, G. (2010). Why 'what works' still won't work: From evidence-based education to value-based education. *Studies in Philosophy and Education, 29*(5), 491–503.

Billett, S. E. (2010). *Learning Through Practice: Models, traditions, orientations and approaches*. London: Springer.

Black, P., & Wiliam, D. (1998). Assessment and classroom learning. *Assessment in Education, 5*(1), 7–71.

Bourdieu, P. (1986). The forms of capital. In J. Richardson (Ed.), *Handbook of Theory and Research for the Sociology of Education* (pp. 241–258). New York: Greenwood.

Bronfenbrenner, U. (1979). *The Ecology of Human Development*. Cambridge, MA: Harvard University Press.

Bukharin, N., & Preobrazhensky, E. (1920). *The ABC of Communism, Chapter 10* [online] Marxists Internet Archive (marxists.org).

Bush, T., & Glover, D. (2003). *School Leadership: Concepts and evidence*. Nottingham: National College for School Leadership.

Bush, T., & Glover, D. (2014). School leadership models: What do we know? *School Leadership & Management, 34*(5), 553–571.

Carr, W., & Kemmis, S. (1986). *Becoming Critical: Education, knowledge and action research*. Lewes: Falmer.

Centre for Education Research and Innovation. (2008). *21st Century Learning: Research, innovation and policy directions from recent OECD analyses*. Paris, France: OECD.

Cervantes-Soon, C. G. (2017). *Juárez Girls Rising: Transformative education in times of dystopia*. Minneapolis, MN: University of Minnesota Press.

Chantiluke, R., Brian Kwoba, B., & Nkopo, A. (2018). *Rhodes Must Fall*. London: Zed Books.

Choi, Á., & Jerrim, J. (2016). The use (and misuse) of PISA in guiding policy reform: The case of Spain. *Comparative Education, 52*(2), 230–245.

Cochrane, T., & Davey, R. C. (2008). Increasing uptake of physical activity: A social ecological approach. *The Journal of the Royal Society for the Promotion of Health, 128*(1), 31–40.

Coffield, F., Moseley, D., Hall, E., & Ecclestone, K. (2004). *Should We Be Using Learning Styles? What research has to say to practice*. London: Learning and Skills Research Centre.

Cohen, L., Manion, L., & Morrison, K. (2017). *Research Methods in Education*, 8th edition. London: Routledge.

Cotton, K. 1988. Classroom Questioning. Portland OR USA: Education North West. [online] http://educationnorthwest.org/resources/classroom-questioning.

Cuban, L. (2001). *Oversold and Underused: Computers in the classroom*. Cambridge, MA: Harvard University Press.

Darling-Hammond, L., Wei, R. C. & Andree, A. 2010. *How High-achieving Countries Develop Great Teachers*. Stanford, CA: Stanford Center for Opportunity Policy in Education.

Dede, C. (2010). Comparing frameworks for 21st century skills. *21st Century Skills: Rethinking How Students Learn, 20*, 51–76.

Defeyter, M., Graham, P. L., Walton, J., & Apicella, T. (2010). News and views: Breakfast clubs: Availability for British schoolchildren and the nutritional, social and academic benefits. *Nutrition Bulletin, 35*(3), 245–253.

Dewey, J. (1910). *How We Think*. London: D. C. Heath & Company [online] http://archive.org/details/howwethink000838mbp.

Doyle, W. (1977). Learning the classroom environment: An ecological analysis. *Journal of Teacher Education, 28*(6), 51–55.

Duffy, J., Warren, K., & Walsh, M. (2001). Classroom interactions: Gender of teacher, gender of student, and classroom subject. *Sex Roles, 45*(9–10), 579–593.

Elliott, J. (1991). *Action Research for Educational Change*. Buckingham: Open University Press.

Engeström, Y., Engeström, R., & Suntio, A. (2002). Can a school community learn to master its own future? An activity-theoretical study of expansive learning among middle school teachers. In G. Wells & G. Claxton (Eds), *Learning for Life in the 21st Century: Sociocultural Perspectives on the Future of Education*. Oxford: Blackwell.

Eraut, M. (2010). Knowledge, working practices and learning. In S. Billet (Ed.), *Learning Through Practice* (pp. 37–58). London: Springer.

Evans, T. (2002). Part-time research students: Are they producing knowledge where it counts? *Higher Education Research and Development, 21*(2), 155–165.

Fan, H., Xu, J., Cai, Z., He, J., & Fan, X. (2017). Homework and students' achievement in math and science: A 30-year meta-analysis, 1986–2015. *Educational Research Review, 20*, 35–54.

Freire, P. (1970). The adult literacy process as cultural action for freedom. *Harvard Educational Review, 40*(2), 205–225.

Freire, P. (1972). *Pedagogy of the Oppressed*. New York: Herder.

Fuchs T., & Wößmann L. (2008) What accounts for international differences in student performance? A re-examination using PISA data. In C. Dustmann, B. Fitzenberger, & S. Machin (Eds) *The Economics of Education and Training* (pp. 209–240). Heidelberg: Springer.

Fullan, M. (2007). *The New Meaning of Educational Change*, 4th edition. New York: Teachers College Press.

Fullan, M., & Langworthy, M. (2013). *Towards a New End: New pedagogies for deep learning*. Seattle, WA: Creative Commons.

Fuller, A., & Unwin, L. (2004). Expansive learning environments: Integrating organizational and personal development. In H. Rainbird, A. Fuller, & A. Munro (Eds), *Workplace Learning in Context* (pp. 126–144). London: Routledge.

Gardiner, S. (2017). Futures loss, despair and empowerment work in the University of Vechta: An action research project. In P. Corcoran, J. Weakland, & A. Wals (Eds), *Envisioning Futures for Environmental and Sustainability Education* (pp. 203–213). Wageningen: Wageningen Academic Publishers.

Gibbs, G. (1988). *Learning by Doing: A guide to teaching and learning methods*. Oxford: Oxford Polytechnic Further Education Unit.

Grenfell, M. (2004). *Pierre Bourdieu: Agent provocateur*. London: Continuum.

Haddad, M., Pinfold, V., Ford, T., Walsh, B., & Tylee, A. (2018). The effect of a training programme on school nurses' knowledge, attitudes, and depression recognition skills: The QUEST cluster randomised controlled trial. *International Journal of Nursing Studies, 83*, 1–10.

Hammond, M. (2018). 'An interesting paper but not sufficiently theoretical': What does theorising in social research look like? *Methodological Innovations, May–August 2018*, 1–10.

Hammond, M., & Wellington, J. (2013). *Research Methods in Education: The key concepts*. London, Routledge.

Hanna, W. (2007). The new Bloom's taxonomy: Implications for music education. *Arts Education Policy Review, 108*(4), 7–16.

Hanushek, E., & Woßmann, L. (2010). Education and economic growth. In E. Peterson & B. McGaw (Eds), *International Encyclopedia of Education Volume 2* (pp. 245–252). Oxford: Elsevier.

Härmä, J. (2009). Can choice promote Education for All? Evidence from growth in private primary schooling in India. *Compare, 39*(2), 151–165.

Hattie, J. (2013). *Visible Learning: A synthesis of over 800 meta-analyses relating to achievement*. London: Routledge.

Hayek, F. (1944). *The Road to Serfdom*. London: Routledge & Kegan Paul.

Haynes, L., Goldacre, B., & Torgerson, D. (2012). *Test, Learn, Adapt: Developing public policy with randomised controlled trials*. London: Cabinet Office.

Higgins, S. (2018). *Improving Learning: Meta-analysis of intervention research in education*. Cambridge: Cambridge University Press.

Hirsch, E. D. (1996). *The Schools We Need: And why we don't have them*. New York: Anchor.

Hollingshead, A., Kroeger, S. D., Altus, J., & Trytten, J. B. (2016). A case study of positive behavior supports-based interventions in a seventh-grade urban classroom. *Preventing School Failure: Alternative Education for Children and Youth, 60*(4), 1–8.

Holt, J. (1964). *How Children Fail*. New York: Pitman Press.

Howard-Jones, P. A. (2014). Neuroscience and education: Myths and messages. *Nature Reviews Neuroscience, 15*, 817–824.

Human Rights: Office of the High Commissioner. (1989). *United Nations Convention on the Rights of the Child*. Geneva, Switzerland: OHCHR [online] www.ohchr.org.

Illich, I. (1973). *Deschooling Society*. Harmondsworth: Marion Boyards Publishers.

Jerrim, J. (2015). Why do East Asian children perform so well in PISA? An investigation of Western-born children of East Asian descent. *Oxford Review of Education, 41*(3), 310–333.

Karoui, K. & Feki, R. (2018). The impacts of gender inequality in education on economic growth in Tunisia: An empirical analysis. *Quality & Quantity, 52*(3), 1265–1273.

Keane, M., Khupe, C., & Sehawer, M. (2017). Decolonising methodology: Who benefits from indigenous knowledge research? *Educational Research for Social Change, 6*(1), 12–24.

Kolb, D. (1984). *Experiential Learning as the Science of Learning and Development.* Englewood Cliffs, NJ: Prentice Hall.

Korpershoek, H., Harms, T., de Boer, H., van Kuijk, M., & Doolaard, S. (2016). A meta-analysis of the effects of classroom management strategies and classroom management programs on students' academic, behavioral, emotional, and motivational outcomes. *Review of Educational Research, 86*(3), 643–680.

Krause, M. (2016). The meanings of theorizing. *The British Journal of Sociology, 67*(1), 23–29.

Kwet, M. (2017). Operation Phakisa Education: Why a secret? Mass surveillance, inequality, and race in South Africa's emerging national e-education system. *First Monday, 22*(12).

Labaree, D. F. (2018). Public schools for private gain: The declining American commitment to serving the public good. *Phi Delta Kappan, 100*(3), 8–13.

Lagemann, E. C. (2002). *An Elusive Science: The troubling history of education research.* Chicago, IL: University of Chicago Press.

Lave, J. (1977). Cognitive consequences of traditional apprenticeship training in West Africa. *Anthropology & Education Quarterly, 8*(3), 177–180.

Lave, J., & Wenger, E. (1991). *Situated Learning: Legitimate peripheral participation.* Cambridge: Cambridge University Press.

Leithwood, K., Harris, A., & Hopkins, D. (2008). Seven strong claims about successful school leadership. *School Leadership and Management, 28*(1), 27–42.

Lemke, J. L. (1990). *Talking Science: Language, learning, and values.* Norwood, NJ: Ablex Publishing Corporation.

Lewin, K. (1997 [1951]). *Resolving Social Conflicts.* Seattle, WA: American Psychological Association.

Littleton, K., Mercer, N., Dawes, L., Wegerif, R., Rowe, D., & Sams, C. (2005). Talking and thinking together at Key Stage 1. *Early Years, 25*(2), 167–182.

Marton, F., Hounsell, D., & Entwistle, N. J. (1997). *The Experience of Learning: Implications for Teaching and Studying in Higher Education.* Edinburgh: Scottish Academic Press.

Marton, F., & Säljö, R. (1976a). On qualitative differences in learning: I – Outcome and process. *British Journal of Educational Psychology, 46*(1), 4–11.

Marton, F., & Säljö, R. (1976b). On qualitative differences in learning: II – Outcome as a function of the learner's conception of the task. *British Journal of Educational Psychology, 46*(2), 115–127.

McGregor, D., & Cartwright, L. (2011). *Developing Reflective Practice: A guide for beginning teachers.* Maidenhead: McGraw-Hill Education.

McNiff, J. (2016). *You and Your Own Action Research Project,* 4th edition. London: Routledge.

Mercer, N. (1995). *The Guided Construction of Knowledge: Talk amongst teachers and learners.* Clevedon: Multilingual Matters.

Mercer, N. (2002). *Words and Minds: How we use language to think together.* London: Routledge.

Mezirow, J. (1997). Transformative learning: Theory to practice. *New Directions for Adult and Continuing Education, 74,* 5–12.

Mishra, P., & Koehler, M. (2007). Technological pedagogical content knowledge (TPCK): Confronting the wicked problems of teaching with technology. In *Society for Information Technology & Teacher Education International Conference,* (pp. 2214–2226). Waynesville, NC: Association for the Advancement of Computing in Education (AACE).

Molfese, D. L., Ivanenko, A., Key, A. F., Roman, A., Molfese, V. J., O'Brien, L., Gozal, D., Kota, S., & Hudac, C. M. (2013). A one-hour sleep restriction impacts brain processing in young children across tasks: Evidence from event-related potentials. *Developmental Neuropsychology, 38*(5), 317–336.

Montessori, M. (1913). *The Montessori Method: Scientific pedagogy as applied to child education in the children's houses* (Translated by A. E. George). New York: Frederick Stokes.

Murphy, M. (2013). *Social Theory and Education Research.* London: Routledge.

Oakeshott, M. (1989). Education: The engagement and its frustration. In T. Fuller (Ed.), *The Voice of Liberal Learning: Michael Oakeshott on education.* New Haven, CT: Yale University Press.

Pestalozzi, J. (1894). *How Gertrude Teaches Her Children: An attempt to help mothers to teach their own children and an account of the method* (Translated by L. Holland & C. Turner). London: George Allen and Unwin.

Plato, & Waterfield, R. (2005). *Meno and Other Dialogues: Charmides, Laches, Lysis, Meno.* Oxford: Oxford University Press.

Pressey, S. L. (1950). Development and appraisal of devices providing immediate automatic scoring of objective tests and concomitant self-instruction. *The Journal of Psychology, 29*(2), 417–447.

Punch, K., & Oancea, A. (2014). *Introduction to Research Methods in Education.* London: Sage.

Reay, D. (2001). Finding or losing yourself? Working-class relationships to education. *Journal of Education Policy, 16*(4), 333–346.

Redfield, D. L., & Rousseau, E. W. (1981). A meta-analysis of experimental research on teacher questioning behavior. *Review of Educational Research, 51*(2), 237–245.

Reese, W. (2001). The origins of progressive education. *History of Education Quarterly, 41,* 1–24.

Repko, A. F., & Szostak, R. (2017). *Interdisciplinary Research: Process and theory.* Thousand Oaks, CA: Sage.

Revans, R. W. (1982). *ABC of Action Learning: Empowering managers to act and to learn from action.* London: Lemons and Crane.

Rogers, B. (2011). *You Know the Fair Rule: Strategies for positive and effective behaviour management and discipline in schools:* Victoria: Australian Council for Educational Research.

Rogers, C. (1969). *Freedom to Learn: A view of what education might become.* New York: C. E. Merrill.

Rowe, M. B. (1974). Wait-time and rewards as instructional variables: Their influence on language, logic, and fate control. *Journal of Research in Science Teaching, 11*(2), 81–94.

Ryan, A. (1995). *John Dewey and the High Tide of American Liberalism.* New York: W. W. Norton and Company.

Ryan, A. (2011). J. S. Mill on education. *Oxford Review of Education, 37*(5), 653–667.

Ryle, G. (1949). *The Concept of Mind.* London: Routledge.

Sahlberg, P. (2011). *Finnish Lessons: What can the world learn from educational change in Finland?* New York: Teachers College Press.

Savage, G. (2017). Neoliberalism, education and curriculum. In B. Gobby & R. Walker (Eds), *Powers of Curriculum: Sociological perspectives on education* (pp. 143–165). New York: Oxford University Press.

Schön, D. A. (1983). *The Reflective Practitioner: How professionals think in action.* London: Temple Smith.

Sclater, N., Webb, M., & Danson, M. (2016). *The Future of Data-Driven Decision Making.* Bristol: JISC.

Sellar, S., Thompson, G., & Rutkowski, D. (2017). *The Global Education Race: Taking the measure of PISA and international testing.* Edmonton: Brush Education.

Sheng, X. (2018). Confucian home education in China. *Educational Review (advance),* 1–18.

Shulman, L. S. (1986). Those who understand: Knowledge growth in teaching. *Educational Researcher, 15*(4), 4–14.

Silberman, R. (2002). An art or a science? *Journal of Education, 183*(2), 13–49.

Söderström, Å., & Löfdahl Hultman, A. (2017). Preschool work against bullying and degrading treatment: Experiences from an action learning project. *Early Years, 37,* 300–312.

Stake, R. (1995). *The Art of Case Study Research.* Thousand Oaks, CA: Sage.

Stigler, J. W., & Hiebert, J. (1999). *The Teaching Gap: Best ideas from the world's teachers for improving education in the classroom.* New York: Summit Books.

Strand, S. (2014). School effects and ethnic, gender and socio-economic gaps in educational achievement at age 11. *Oxford Review of Education, 40*(2), 223–245.

Strauss, A., & Corbin, J. (1990). *Basics of Qualitative Research*. Thousand Oaks, CA: Sage.

Stringer, E., McFadyen, L., & Baldwin, S. (2010). *Integrating Teaching, Learning and Action Research: Enhancing instruction in the K–12 classroom*. Thousand Oaks, CA: Sage.

Stylianou, P., & Zembylas, M. (2018). Peer support for bereaved children: Setting eyes on children's views through an educational action research project. *Death Studies, 42*(7), 446–455.

Thomas, G. (2016). *How to Do Your Case Study*. Thousand Oaks, CA: Sage.

Thorndike, E. L. (1913). *The Psychology of Learning* (Vol. 2). New York: Teachers College Press.

Tooley, J., & Dixon, P. (2005). *Private Education Is Good for The Poor: A study of private schools serving the poor in low-income countries*. Washington, DC: Cato Institute.

Toothaker, R. (2018). Millennial's perspective of clicker technology in a nursing classroom: A mixed methods research study. *Nurse Education Today, 62*, 80–84.

Torgerson, C. (2003). *Systematic Reviews*. London: Bloomsbury.

Truong, T. D., & Hallinger, P. (2017). Exploring cultural context and school leadership: conceptualizing an indigenous model of có uy school leadership in Vietnam. *International Journal of Leadership in Education, 20*(5), 539–561.

Walsh, J. A., & Sattes, B. D. (2016). *Quality Questioning: Research-based practice to engage every learner*. Thousand Oaks, CA: Corwin Press.

Wellington, J. (2015). *Educational Research: Contemporary issues and practical approaches*. London: Bloomsbury Academic.

Wenger, E. (1998). *Communities of Practice: Learning, meaning, and identity*. Cambridge: Cambridge University Press.

Whitehead, J. (1989). Creating a living educational theory from questions of the kind, 'How do I improve my practice?'. *Cambridge Journal of Education, 19*(1), 41–52.

Williamson, B. (2017). *Big Data in Education: The digital future of learning, policy and practice*. London: Sage.

Willis, P. (1977). *Learning to Labour: How working class kids get working class jobs*. London: Routledge.

Winter, R. (1989). *Learning From Experience: Principles and practice in action-research*. London: The Falmer Press.

Yoshida, M. (1999). *Lesson Study: An ethnographic investigation of school-based teacher development in Japan* (Doctoral dissertation). University of Chicago, Chicago.

Yousafzai, M., & McCormick, P. (2014). *I am Malala: How one girl stood up for education and changed the world*. London: Weidenfeld & Nicolson.

INDEX